Hallowed Ground

The Folklore of Churches and Churchyards

About the Author

Mark Norman is a folklorist and author based in Devon, in the South West of the UK. He is the curator of the Folklore Library and Archive, a council member of the Folklore Society, and the creator and host of The Folklore Podcast. Ranked in the top half percent of podcasts in its genre around the world, and with around two million downloads behind it, The Folklore Podcast is recognized as one of the leading shows in the field of folklore today.

Hallowed Ground

The Folklore of Churches and Churchyards

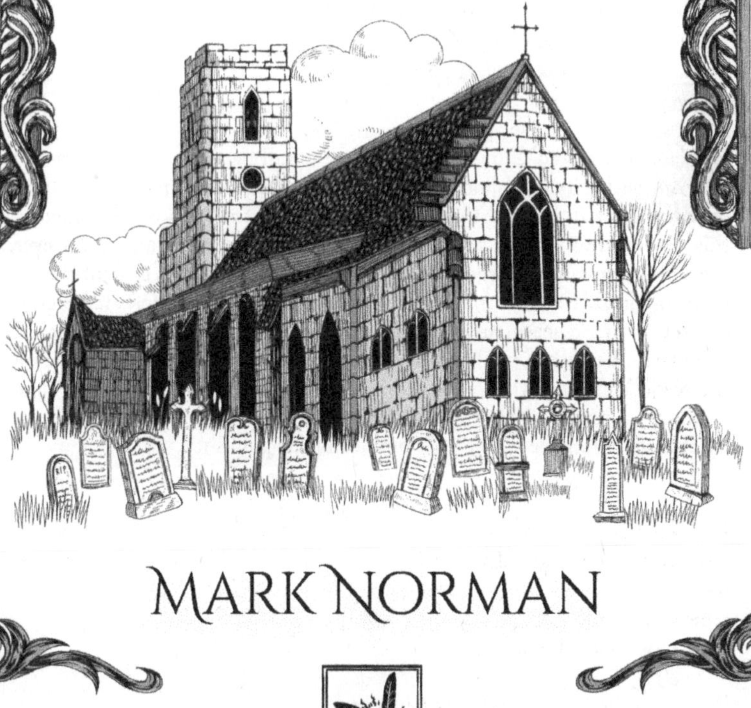

Mark Norman

Chicago, Illinois

Paperback ISBN: 978-1-964537-00-9
Hardcover ISBN: 978-1-964537-30-6
Library of Congress Control Number on file.

Published by:
Crossed Crow Books, LLC
6934 N Glenwood Ave, Suite C
Chicago, IL 60626
www.crossedcrowbooks.com

Printed in the United States of America.
IBI

OTHER TITLES BY THE AUTHOR

ZOINKS!: The Spooky Folklore Behind Scooby Doo
(Oak Tree Books, 2024)

Dark Folklore (The History Press, 2024)

The Folklore of Wales: Ghosts (Calon, 2024)

The Folklore of Devon (University of Exeter Press, 2024)

Telling the Bees and Other Customs:
The Folklore of Rural Crafts (The History Press, 2020)

Black Dog Folklore (Troy Books Publishing, 2016)

CONTENTS

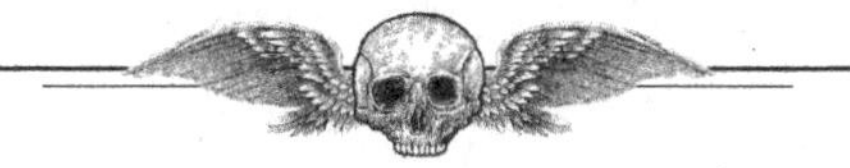

INTRODUCTION

"The curfew tolls the knell of parting day,
The lowing herd wind slowly o'er the lea,
The ploughman homeward plods his weary way,
And leaves the world to darkness and to me.

Now fades the glimmering landscape on the sight,
And all the air a solemn stillness holds,
Save where the beetle wheels his droning flight,
And drowsy tinklings lull the distant folds:

Save that from yonder ivy-mantled tow'r
The moping owl does to the moon complain
Of such, as wand'ring near her secret bow'r,
Molest her ancient solitary reign."

These words, written in the mid-eighteenth century—probably around 1742—by Thomas Gray are the opening of a piece of poetry titled "Elegy Written in a Country Churchyard." In the poem, the unnamed speaker begins by describing the sights and sounds of the peaceful country churchyard in which he sits. The verses paint a picture of the stereotype of a traditional, quaint village church and graveyard which would sit in the heart of most rural communities.

As the poem unfolds, Gray moves away from these images and begins to muse of life's wasted opportunities, then ultimately upon death itself. This is something which affected the author himself and drove him to question his own mortality. In short, the poem becomes much darker. This is the aesthetic that we will be adopting throughout this book as we explore the church and churchyard in terms of its folklore, superstition, and magic.

It's important to be clear from the very start as to what this book is and how it approaches the subject matter. Religion and the Church can be a divisive topic for many, and issues of belief and faith should command a certain amount of respect. It is likely that, throughout history, more wars have been fought in the name of religion than for any other reason. However, as a folklorist—much as with exploration of topics of the paranormal, cryptozoology, or other areas outside of the bounds of hard science—it is not my place to question whether something exists or not.

Folklore is concerned with how people's beliefs and experiences give them a sense of place and identity in the world, and what the shared beliefs of a folk group mean for that group and others who interact with them. This was best described to me once through the phrase "folklore is neutral." That sentiment should sit at the heart of this discussion. *Hallowed Ground* aims to explore the beliefs, traditions, and superstitions connected with the church and the churchyard through the lens of folklore and not with an opinion on any particular religion.

It is impossible to say for certain how many churches and places of worship there are in the world. In the United Kingdom—where I live—there are a little over forty thousand. The National Churches Trust points out that this is greater than the number of pubs in the country—although this number also includes sacred spaces, such as Stonehenge. The number of Anglican churches stands at around sixteen thousand.

Extrapolating this figure across the globe is complex. In some countries, churches are not required to register with the government. No official census has ever been conducted. At the broadest level, we can even question what constitutes a church. Looking at the Christian faith (bearing in mind there are as many organisations and denominations of that worldwide as there are places of worship in the UK), we can use mathematics to give a rough idea. Working with the suggestion that there are a little under one hundred congregants in the average church and that there are around 2.18 billion Christians across the planet, this would leave us with a staggering twenty-seven million Christians meeting at different locations.

I suspect that the fine people at Crossed Crow Books would be a little grumpy if I tried to put together an examination on this scale, as the cost of shipping on a book of that size would be on the higher end of the scale. The point here is that this book can only ever be a small cross-section of the wealth of potential material that could be examined when we delve into the fascinating world of folklore in connection with our churches. Therefore, we need to narrow the field down a little.

Hallowed Ground will concentrate on the church in Western Christianity, with its main focus being on the United Kingdom and United States. Other locations and faiths are used for the purposes of comparison; however, to treat any other faith fairly, it would need its own book.

With all that clear in our minds, let's begin this exploration of the folklore of our churches and churchyards with a look at the church building itself. What did—and does—the church mean to the community that grows around it? How did it get there in the first place? I'm sure it's probably fairies...

CHAPTER ONE

THE CONSTRUCTION AND ROLE OF THE CHURCH

FOLKLORE IS ALL ABOUT COMMUNITY. We are all members of folk groups—gathering places where people can enjoy shared interests. The church is somewhat similar—it has a role as a spiritual centre and a place for worship and devotion, but it also acts as a focal point for the community—a social space. It is both a place of celebration and a place to seek sanctuary, guidance, or help in times of tragedy or loss. The church is many things to many people.

Historically, the church stood at the very centre of a community. It was expected that most, if not all, of the community would be there on a Sunday. Today, attendee numbers are dwindling, and the average age of the congregation is much higher than it once was. Many may argue that the Church no longer has the relevance it once did. However, we should not be too quick to dismiss it entirely.

The numbers quoted at the end of this book's introduction show that the Church is not going away any time soon. However, its role is shifting and developing in the modern world. The modern Church might provide much more than just spiritual sustenance. It might host food banks, charity bake sales, act as a polling station, or even have a local shop. Closure of church buildings is avoided whenever possible.

A 2023 study by the University of Birmingham highlights the church building as an "anchor institution," the terminology used for any organisation that holds a vital presence in a community and for which the community's well-being would suffer if it were to close.

The study gives two examples from the English county of Norfolk. In the first, St Mary's Church in Bessingham, a trust keeps the building open, despite it only providing six services a year. In the other example, a church is able to keep its doors open despite providing no worship services at all. The eleventh-century All Saints' Church in Waterden is cared for by a community group who raised funds to restore the structure and reopen it to the public, where it can now be visited and enjoyed once again.

These are not isolated examples, however. Organisations such as the Historic Chapels Trust and the Churches Conservation Trust (which All Saints' Church now sits under) have saved many more. While these buildings may no longer hold formal religious services, they still play a vital role in their communities.

It is apparent, then, that we can think about the church building both in physical brick-and-mortar terms and in the building of its role and the community. But let's begin with the structure itself.

When we consider the construction of the church, for the most part, we aren't thinking about the physical or architectural processes involved—although the odd grotesque, gargoyle, or other adornment will rear its head during the course of this book. Rather, we are turning to folklore to look for explanations for some of the more unusual aspects of raising a church. One of these can often be found in the location of the building itself.

Throughout history, there have been many instances where the spread of Christianity subsumed Pagan structures and worship sites into the construction of its church buildings. Some examples of this are particularly well known: the Pantheon in Rome was originally dedicated to the Roman gods before it was converted to a Roman Catholic church; St Peter's Basilica, contained within Vatican City and considered to be one of the most holy shrines of the Catholic Church, being the alleged burial place of St Peter himself, was built on top of Roman mausoleums which were part of a larger necropolis, according to evidence put forwards by archaeological exploration there. The same thing happened across Europe. It was said of the French saint, Martin of Tours, that "wherever he destroyed heathen temples, there he used immediately to build either churches or monasteries."

In the United Kingdom, it isn't always quite so clear-cut. There are certainly plenty of sites across the country where the archaeological record demonstrates that they have been places of worship since Anglo-Saxon times—that is, the period between AD 410 and 1066. These centuries used to be known as the "Dark Ages," referring to the lack of written sources covering this time. Many historians now tend to use "Early Middle Ages" or "early medieval" as preferred terms.

In much the same way that a lot of rubbish has been published on social media about the Pagan roots of every Christian celebration and ritual imaginable, research seems to suggest that it was actually quite unusual in England for churches to grow out of Pagan temples—at least until somewhere around the sixth century. That means that there were approximately six hundred years where there was at least some co-existence of old and new religions.

While many holy places in the country's landscape are now gone, some still exist. For example, we have a proliferation of holy wells. Some of these are now associated with saints, but plenty still have names that hark back to older times. The practice of "well-dressing," in which wells and springs are adorned with artistic designs created from foliage and flower petals, still takes place at some of these sites each Whitsuntide. Whitsun, or Whit Sunday (a contraction of White Sunday with reference to the Biblical Holy Ghost), is the name used across Britain for the Holy Day of Pentecost, the seventh Sunday after Easter. Whitsuntide describes the week which follows this Sunday. Again, while many sources posit that this ritual stems from the Pagans making sacrifices to water deities, the true origins cannot be traced any earlier than the fourteenth century and the decoration of the well at Tissington in Derbyshire. The most-likely scenario is that this was done to give thanks for the fresh water that the well provided, either during a period of drought or because of a belief that the purity of the water was a factor in surviving the second great plague that started with the Black Death.

There are two predominant reasons why sacred wells would have become established. Either the waters would be said to have healing properties, or they would be considered suitable for divination. Even those wells which became attached to Christian saints still managed to retain these magical properties, although they would then tend to be referred to as "miraculous" rather than magical. St Agnes Well, in the English county of Somerset, became very well-known because Henrietta, wife of King Charles I, was said to have wished for a child there and then subsequently fell pregnant.

Offerings would often be made at these holy wells. In many cases, the offering would take the form of a bent pin (we find a number of "pin wells" across Britain). Sometimes, offerings would be much more spectacular and valuable. One might draw a parallel here with the modern day "wishing well." Tokens would often be left behind as part of the magic. This happened frequently in Scotland, where many wells became known as "clootie wells"—*clootie* meaning "cloth" in the Scots' dialect and cloth rags being the most common item to be left as an offering. Now, we often see clooties tied to tree branches.

The intersection between the Christian faith and these more magical ideas was not an uncommon one, as we will see in more detail in Chapter Five when we explore the topic of magic and Witchcraft in connection with the Church.

There is plenty of evidence found in folklore to suggest that many Christian missionaries chose not to remove heathen beliefs from everyday rhetoric. After all, there was nothing to gain from alienating those who they were ultimately trying to covert to their religion. The Church authorities, however, often took a somewhat stronger view. In AD 567, for example, a decree was put out at the time of the Council of Tours that proclaimed: "with[sic] respect to trees, stones and fountains, where certain foolish people light torches or practice other superstitions, we earnestly ordain that the most evil[sic] custom, detestable to God, wherever it is found, should be removed and destroyed."

This depiction of some members of the community as "foolish" by the higher-class and (at least in their own minds) "enlightened" clergy carries forwards into the nineteenth-century collection of folklore by antiquarian scholars, often clergymen themselves, and their descriptions of the "uneducated" and "superstitious" rural common folk. Their legacy of employing such terminology still introduces bias in folklore material to this day.

Returning to the folklore surrounding the construction of the church, a common recurring story, or trope, tells how a number of churches were supposed to be built in one location, but actually ended up somewhere else. Often, this is a church which was supposed to be on top of a hill, but every night the Devil would come and throw all the stones back to the bottom. In the end, the builders relented and put their church at the bottom instead.

Sometimes the story is the other way round. The church is on top of a hill, or is located some distance from a settlement, which makes getting to it more awkward. The stories have, therefore, developed over time to account for the unexpected locations. This is the case, for example, at the very remote Brentor Church on Dartmoor in West Devon, a working church believed to be located on the highest point in southern England. Dedicated to St Michael de Rupe, the iconic building was founded in 1130 by Robert Giffard, a local landowner. The building's facade as it looks now developed over the following two hundred years from the original chantry chapel that stood atop the hill.

Folklore tells a different story. The Devil had been unable to claim any souls from Dartmoor for a long while. So, when a merchant ship was seen arriving in the English Channel from the spice routes, he created a huge storm which blew out the beacon that burned on Brentor (which used to be known as "Beacon Tor"). The captain of the ship battled bravely all night to keep the vessel from sinking, but, by the morning, believed that all was lost. On board, the merchant, Hugh, prayed to his patron saint, Michael, vowing that if the ship was saved, he would build a church on the highest land that he could find once getting ashore and dedicate it to him. Instantly, the storm subsided, and the ship was saved.

Hugh was good to his word and began building the church on top of the highest land that he sighted: Brentor. That night, the Devil passed by and was incensed by the construction, so he flung all the stone to the bottom of the hill. However, Hugh was determined and drug everything back to the top of the hill the next day to recommence. This went on for weeks before St Michael noticed what was happening and stepped in to help.

The next night, when the Devil arrived, he found Michael waiting for him. The saint picked up a granite boulder and threw it after the now-rapidly retreating Devil, hitting him on the heel. Being incapacitated for some time, the Devil stayed away, and Hugh was able to complete his construction.

On the surface, this is a fine story with many of the elements that we find at other churches. However, what is the main sticking point here? The story tells how Hugh chooses Brentor because it is the "first and highest point of land" sighted after the storm. The port of Plymouth, feeding into the English Channel, on the south coast of Devon is over twenty miles from Brentor, and Hugh would have had to cross a large swathe of Dartmoor to reach it—not exactly the first point of land he would have sighted, unless he walked there with his eyes closed.

In my book *The Folklore of Devon*, I discuss the impact of what I term "guidebook folklore" on tourist areas. Stemming from the development of the railways in the nineteenth century, which coincided with a flourishing of interest in folklore, many tourist books published at this time used romanticised and embellished versions of local stories to capture the imagination of visitors to the area. The Devil at Brentor may possibly have this sort of origin as well.

The Church of St Mary the Virgin at East Bergholt in Suffolk is notable for its unusual bell house, which is separated from the main church. Construction of an actual bell tower began here in 1525. However, after the fall of Cardinal Wolsey at the hands of Henry VIII, money he had promised the church was significantly reduced. In 1531, as what was supposed to be a temporary solution, the Bell Cage was erected, and it remains in use to this day. It is the only bell tower known where the bells are still rung by pulling on a wooden headstock, rather than the more common ropes and wheels found in most belfries.

However, legend tells us that it was not a lack of funds but interference by the Devil that led to the wooden Bell Cage instead of the stone tower.

This architectural disruption by the forces of Hell acts as a commentary of the power of the Church in overcoming evil. However, we should also remember that in folklore, particularly those stories relating to the landscape and the features within it, the Devil is merely a more modern replacement for other figures who came before. Many an erratic rock that was said to have been tossed there by the Devil during a fight has an older tale attached to it describing how a giant did it and ran away.

We will be exploring many more of these stories surrounding the Devil in Chapter Six, but, for now, we shouldn't have to wait to include a particularly entertaining version from Germany. According to legend, the Devil arrived in the German city of Lübeck in the thirteenth century because he had noticed that a new church was being built there. This was the Gothic Basilica of St Mary's (which was notably almost completely destroyed in an air raid on Palm Sunday in 1942, but was subsequently reconstructed).

The labourers constructing the church were, naturally, very frightened of the Devil's presence and, therefore, would not admit to building a church. Instead, they told him that they were working on an impressive wine bar. This pleased the Devil, who expected that it would send many sinners his way, so he pitched in and lent a hand—or rather a hoof—to the workers.

Of course, they couldn't hide the shape of the building forever. When the Devil finally realised, he was very annoyed. He grabbed the nearest slab of stone and was about to throw it at the church when a quick-thinking builder stepped up and placated the Devil by assuring him that they would still build a wine bar after the church was finished. This made the Devil much happier, and he dropped the slab beside the church.

Known today as "the Devil's Stone," the slab bears indentations which are said to resemble the claw marks that were left behind when he picked up the stone. A recently added small statue of the Devil now sits atop the stone, and as promised, there is a tavern on the opposite side of the road.

We find very similar stories to these in the disrupted construction of churches relating to the fairy folk in different forms as well. For example, at Tingwell, on the Shetland Isles to the far north of Scotland, it was decided that a broch would be dismantled and the stone used for building a church. A broch is a kind of prehistoric drystone-walled tower found both on the Shetland and Orkney islands, as well as the Scottish mainland. The name derives from the lowland Scots' word *brough,* meaning "fort," and the structure is generally made up of two concentric walls which enclose a courtyard and apartments. However, the intention to use the stone in this way upsets the Trows in the area.

Trows are a particular type of sprite which are native to these islands. They look somewhat like humans in appearance, but are typically uglier and smaller, although there are examples of Trows described as giants found as well. They favour habitats inland from the coast, where the ground is made up of peat and cause trouble amongst humans nocturnally. Trows are not found at large during the day because they share a particular characteristic with the Scandinavian trolls to the north. That is, if they are not concealed underground before the sun rose, they would turn to stone. This is said to account for a number of the menhirs and standing stones found on the islands.

The Trows objected to an ancient structure such as the broch being misused in order to construct a church; so, every night, they would undo the work which had been done during the day. This take is different to those in which the structure is relocated elsewhere because of the disruption. At Tingwell, a priest was brought in to consecrate the ground, driving the Trows away, causing them to relocate to another nearby island.

A similar story can be found in England at Stowe-Nine-Churches, where bad planning on someone's part led to the attempted construction of a church on the site of a fairy ring. Naturally, the fairy folk were not pleased and dug out the foundation each night. In an attempt to combat this, a monk decided to stay overnight at the location. Once he saw the fairies and realised that it was definitely them to blame, he immediately began to pray for their removal.

It does seem that not all of the fairies would interfere with construction, however. If the price was right, they might do the work for you. There are a large number of sites in Scotland which folklore says were built by fairies. Amongst these is the Church of St Mary's at Dundee, which was apparently built for gold.

Some stories are much darker. Nonna, or Non, was the mother of St David, the patron saint of Wales, and lived in the fifth century. There are a few variations to her story, but the prominent tradition tells that her son was the product of her having been assaulted, possibly by Sanctus, the King of Ceredigion, although other rulers have been named. It was predicted that her unborn child would become a great preacher, as a local vicar had found themselves unable to deliver a sermon in the presence of a pregnant Non. This story reached the ear of the local ruler, who feared the potential power of the yet unborn child, and so he hatched a plot to kill David at birth.

On the day that Non went into labour, a great storm rose up which had such ferocity that it prevented anyone from travelling. Legend says that the pain of childbirth was so intense that Non left nail marks in a rock that she had grabbed during her labour. This action caused the rock to split apart. A chapel, named the Chapel of St Non, was built on this site and the two halves of the rock were said to have been used for the foundations of the altar there. Only ruins remain of this original chapel now, although another bearing the name of the Chapel of Our Lady and St Non was built nearby in 1934. Also close by is Non's holy well.

Other wells named for Non can be found in Cornwall, in South West England, where it has been suggested that she travelled after these events took place. One is at Pelynt, meaning "the place of Non," and another at Altarnun, "the altar of Non." Her relics were venerated here at one time, before the Reformation brought about their destruction.

Assuming that one has actually managed to avoid the Devil, the fairy folk, and anyone else who might want to get in the way, folklore still very much comes into play once one has actually managed to get a church built in the first place. Many churches have unusual exterior features—aside from the gargoyles, grotesques, and other waterspouts that we will examine later—and all of these features have folkloric tales attached to them to explain how they came to be.

Several churches have unusually shaped spires. To many, this isn't any great surprise as the spire—used most commonly in Gothic churches, although found in different forms on other church designs too—was one of the more difficult elements of the church to construct. It was certainly prone to damage or collapse.

The church spire, in addition to providing a visually impressive top to the building, acted as a symbol of the human desire to reach Heaven. The construction of this structure began in the twelfth century as a more straightforward pyramid roof atop the tower, before developing over time to the slim structures that are expected now. People often use the terms *spire* and *steeple* interchangeably, favouring steeple in smaller country churches and spire on grander urban structures. However, in terms of architecture, there is a distinction to be made, as a steeple refers to a series of building stories which get gradually smaller as they get higher, topped off by a small spire.

The complex nature of the construction of the spire leads to stories developing, especially when it has a look which differs from the norm. Sometimes, there are a number of different stories which may change over time. Take, for instance, the Church of St Mary and All Saints in Chesterfield, Derbyshire. This is another church with a long lineage. There is evidence of Christian worship on the church site since Anglo-Saxon times, and the building contains a font which is believed to date from the first century AD.

The construction of this church as we see it today began in 1234, although the majority of building took place in the fourteenth century. The spire, in this case, was added in 1362. It stands 228 feet above the ground at its point, and today forms a significant corkscrew shape, although the sides would have been straight at the time that it was built.

A number of practical theories have been put forward for the spire's subsequent twist (which is some forty-five degrees) and its lean of almost three metres off-centre. These include using unseasoned timber, the addition of thirty-three tonnes of lead sheet (which the spire is now clad in), uneven expansion of that same lead due to the sun's position to the south, and a lack of workers in the fourteenth century with sufficient skill to construct it in the first place due to the impact of the plague.

Naturally, the folklore is far more exciting in its reasoning, and most of it involves the Devil in some way. Maybe it was due to a local blacksmith who was fitting a horseshoe to the Devil's foot, hammering a nail into the soft part of his flesh by accident. The Devil, hopping all over the town in pain, knocked the spire as he passed.

This story does seem to borrow from a number of folk stories more generally involving a blacksmith shoeing the Devil. There are a great many of these—the folk tale of "The Blacksmith and the Devil" having been shown to be one of the oldest in the world—and a number of this story's variations provide explanation for how the smith got his skills. Later versions tie the role of the smith with the Christian saint Dunstan, once Archbishop of Glastonbury. When the Devil turned up at Dunstan's smithy and asked for his horse to be reshod, Dunstan nailed the shoes to the Devil instead. This caused a lot of pain, and the saint made the Devil promise that he would never enter a house with a horseshoe on the door before he removed the shoes again. This is why it is considered good luck to hang a horseshoe over a threshold.

Maybe there is another explanation for the twisted spire at St Mary and All Saints. Maybe it is from the time that the Devil sat on top of the spire and wrapped his tail around it. When the town bellringers arrived and pealed the bells, the Devil became alarmed and tried to flee while his tail was still wrapped around the spire, causing it to twist as he ran.

Perhaps it is the story that has him sitting on the spire, with the smell of burning incense wafting up from the church below, causing the Devil to sneeze that explains the twist. Or maybe the one in which he is sitting up there when a bride arrives at the church for her wedding and he twists to watch her as she enters the building.

This last story is particularly interesting (and amusing) because it has been adapted over time—probably by the residents of a nearby town—to provide a commentary on the girls of Chesterfield, where the church is located. In this version, a virgin gets married in the church and the building itself is so surprised that the spire twists round to get a good look at her. Legend says that if another virgin is ever to wed in the church, the spire will twist back the other way to look at her, too. Supposedly, that is the reason why it is still not straight after all this time.

Several churches have spires which appear to have been cut short and never reach their point. Generally, this happens when the money raised for construction of the spire runs out before the job can be completed. In terms of the folklore associated with these structures, a common theme is that of two builders or stonemasons who end up falling to their deaths from the church tower, usually after a quarrel.

A fine example of this can be found at the Church of All Saints in the Leicestershire town of Beeby. The particularly squat top to the church tower here has become known as Beeby's Tub (from Beeby Stub, no doubt) and has this trope attached to it, and the events are celebrated in a local rhyme:

Beeby Tub without a pub,
A church without a spire.
Two brothers fought and broke their backs
And so 'twas built no higher.

If the outside walls of churches are adorned with sculptures, then these will, typically, be in the form of the Christian saints. There are obvious exceptions to this rule, such as gargoyles and grotesques—two different things, despite being interchangeable in many people's minds. Gargoyles began to appear on the designs of European churches in the thirteenth century, and they serve a very specific purpose, being decorative waterspouts. They channel rainwater out from the rooftops and away from the stone walls, thus protecting them from erosion. A gargoyle becomes a grotesque when it serves no purpose other than being placed on the building as a piece of architectural adornment.

It has been suggested that gargoyles are connected to the French legend of a dragon-like monster called *La Gargouille* which once threatened the country around the Rouen area. The dragon was finally defeated by St Romanus, the bishop of Rouen at the time of the mid-first century AD. In different versions of the story, Romanus either vanquished the creature using a crucifix or otherwise with the help of the only person who could be found who would assist—a man who was already condemned to death.

After it was killed, the body of the *Gargouille* was taken to Rouen to be burned. However, because it was a fire-breathing animal, the head and neck could not be destroyed by the fire. Instead, they were hung on the church for protection and to serve as a warning to any other potential monstrous threat.

There are problems to be found with this legend being posited for the origin of the architectural gargoyle by name. First, *Gargouille* was not the only name by which this creature was known, as it was also referred to as *Goji*. Second, this legend has all the hallmarks of a Christianised retrofit for a pre-existing story, in much the same way as the legend of St George and the Dragon (which is not a million miles away in its construction) has also changed and developed over time.

It is possible that this happened because there was already some dissent within the church to the use of gargoyles and grotesques as an image even before they started to become common on the outsides of buildings. Twelfth-century Church Leader St Bernard of Clairvaux had already made his views on the subject very plain when asked:

> *"what[sic] are these fantastic monsters doing in the cloisters before the eyes of the brothers as they read? To what purpose are here placed these creatures? I see several bodies with one head and several heads with one body. Here is a quadruped with a serpent's head, there a fish with a quadruped's head. Surely if we do not blush for such absurdities, we should at least regret what we have spent on them."*

It is far more likely that the word gargoyle derives from the French words *garge,* meaning "to gurgle" and *goule,* or "throat," a perfectly good description of what the stone heads actually do.

Some gargoyles and grotesques added to church buildings today take on a very modern twist, and for this reason may become a part of the folklore of tomorrow. The National Cathedral in Washington, DC, has more than ninety examples created by artist Walter S. Arnold, including robots, a figure wearing a gas mask, and a fly holding a can of Raid. When the twelfth-century Paisley Abbey in Scotland was renovated in 1991, twelve gargoyles had to be replaced. One of the new designs installed was fashioned after the xenomorph designed by Swiss artist H.R. Giger for the *Alien* movie franchise.

Gargoyles are not the only adornment to a church that you would expect holy men like St Bernard to get their cassock in a flap about. There are numerous examples of both figures and other apparel on the insides of churches that you might not expect to see there. For example, a number of churches were alleged to have Daneskins—a covering of a church door which was said to have been made by flaying the skin of a captured Dane or other intruder from the Scandinavian region.

The north door of Worcester Cathedral was said to be lined with the skin of such a robber who tried to plunder from the high altar. The London landmark Westminster Abbey has a door in the south transept that John Dart described in his 1723 book *History of the Abbey Church of St Peter's, Westminster* as being lined "with skins like parchment."

Many things in folklore, sadly, are not as they first appear, and such is the case for Daneskins. The north door of St Botolph's Church in Hadstock, Essex, was said to still have attached to it a scrap of Viking skin flayed from a marauder who had broken into the church. In 2001, a small sample of it underwent analysis for a television programme made by the British Broadcasting Corporation called *Blood of the Vikings*. The results were not conclusive, but were highly suggestive that the DNA profile was more bovine than human. A more recent retesting by the University of Cambridge using a more sophisticated method of analysis confirmed that the scrap was definitely cowhide and not human in origin.

The earliest-known book giving guidance on the building of churches and the artistic crafts required to do so is *On Divers Arts,* written by Theophilus Presbyter, a pseudonym for a still-anonymous monk born around the year 1070. Amongst the instructions in this three-volume work is instruction on how wooden doors should be covered with animal hide, then subsequently smoothed off and whitened. This technique was designed to highlight to full effect the intricate ironwork used on the door furniture and for adornment.

Often, as we have already seen, churches rise out of older sites of worship. Sometimes, the location for the construction of a church might be decided upon in order to best serve an area of habitation that has grown over time. However, occasionally, the decision is left to little more than chance. Such it was with the legend attached to the Catholic saint Wolfgang of Regensburg.

Wolfgang was born in Swabia, Germany, around the year 934, and was ordained into the faith by St Ulrich in 968. After Emperor Otto II appointed him to the position of Bishop of Regensburg four years later, Wolfgang spent many years both preaching and developing a reputation as a teacher and reformer. In his later life, the saint chose to live to life of a hermit in Austria, and it was from this period that the legend emerges.

It was said that St Wolfgang became determined to build a church, possibly after seeing a vision or dreaming of a particular building. In order to choose the best spot at which to lay the foundations, Wolfgang climbed the Schafberg Mountain and threw down an axe, stating that wherever it landed would be the place for the church to be built. The saint found the axe in an outcrop between the mountain and the lake.

Building a church was no task for Wolfgang alone, so he had to seek help. First, he stopped a wolf who was running past and asked for assistance, but the wolf refused, as it was being pursued by a hunter. When the hunter arrived at the site, St Wolfgang asked him for help as well. Again, he was refused, as the hunter's quarry was not only close in front, but he said he was being dogged by something evil and could not stay long at this place.

Sure enough, before much more time had passed, the Devil walked up to Wolfgang. This time, the saint was able to get help, but, naturally, the Devil came at a price. He was to claim the first soul that set foot in the church. Wolfgang agreed, because, for him, getting the church built to the glory of God was more important than anything else.

It did not take long once the Devil got involved, and soon the church was constructed. The time had come for the Devil to claim his soul. At this point, Wolfgang heard the sound of a hunting horn. The hunter was returning, still chasing the wolf. The saint threw open the church door and the wolf dashed inside, becoming the first living thing to enter. The Devil was furious, knowing that he had been tricked; yet, he still had a soul to claim. He strode into the church, snatched up the wolf, and left, slamming the church door with such force that the metal ring was split in two. The crack remained for all to see.

By no means is this a unique story idea. We see the Devil tricked in this way in folklore on many occasions. The most common motif here surrounds the construction of new bridges where a bargain has to be made, and the bridge can only be built on the understanding that the Devil may claim the first soul to cross the new structure. Usually, a dog is driven across before any human sets foot on the bridge.

A similar method of site selection is found in Scotland, associated with the Church of Fordoun in Kincardineshire. This church was originally intended to be built on Knock Hill, which lies about a mile to the northeast of the village, but its construction was plagued by interference from fairies, or some other unseen spirit in the manner, described earlier in this chapter. In her book *British Folk Tales,* the well-known folklorist Katherine Briggs notes that the new site for the church was chosen by a mason throwing his hammer at random.

The idea of the Devil being tricked into helping with church construction exists in other countries, too. The South American country of Ecuador has one placed in the city of Quito, where it remains one of the area's best-known legends.

Here, San Francisco Cathedral overlooks a plaza of the same name. The building was one of the first churches to be built in Quito, being completed in 1680 after a period of around a century. Legend says that a prominent local builder and architect named Cantuña was commissioned to build the cathedral's atrium. This had to be completed by a certain date or—according to the version of the story told—Cantuña would not be paid and may be jailed.

At the eleventh hour, as it became apparent that this deadline would not be met, the Devil appeared to Cantuña and offered a bargain of the usual nature. He and his demons would finish the construction job overnight, but, in return, he would get the architect's soul. Cantuña had no choice but to accept.

The church was indeed finished, but then Cantuña faced a new dilemma. How would he save his soul? There are a number of different solutions to this provided in different retellings of the legend, but they all revolve around the removal of a piece of stone from the atrium.

In some versions, the builder himself removes and hides a piece of stone from one of the walls, and then points out to the Devil that he cannot claim his soul because the building is not complete. The Devil realises he has been tricked and disappears angrily back to the underworld. In another version, more supportive of the Church's battle over evil, an angel appears and undertakes the stone removal. In a third, Cantuña removes the stone, but, rather than hiding it, he writes a message on it reading that whoever picks up the stone acknowledges that God is greater than himself. The Devil, of course, would not pick up the stone.

A fascinating variation is found in the German city of Munich's Frauenkirche. A footprint at the entrance to the nave here is said to belong to the Devil, who made a similar bargain with this building's architect, only this time with the deal being that the building had to be constructed with no windows. Of course, the cathedral does have windows, but at this exact point none of them can be seen. They are all obscured by pillars, with the main stained-glass piece being hidden behind the altarpiece from this viewpoint.

Whichever version of the story we go with, what we see here is just another reflection of the idea of the Devil being tricked into helping with something in the same way as the story of St Wolfgang and so many others across folklore, whether they refer to religious buildings, bridges, or any other community dilemma. All of them align with the ancient folktale of the Blacksmith and the Devil, which explains how the smith gained his skills in metalwork

Interestingly, the motif of stone removal can also be found in old superstitions surrounding the replacement of church buildings with newer structures. In Aberdeenshire, Scotland, it was believed, for example, that whoever removed the first stone from the old building would be met with a violent death. Because of this, none of the labourers employed to rebuild an old church on a country estate would start the job, and it fell to the estate agent to take out the first stone for them so that work could begin. The suggestion here, which we find across so much folklore of the period, is that the more highly educated agent would not have held the same superstitious beliefs as the common labourers. Unfortunately, history has not recorded what happened to him after removing the stone.

As we saw at the beginning of this chapter, the roles of the church in a community are multifarious in the twenty-first century, but, historically, the spiritual wellbeing of the parishioners was key and formed its main focus. The church building and clergy would fulfil this role in life, and the churchyard would provide safe and consecrated ground in which those parishioners could rest upon in death.

Regular worship was expected, and folklore often explains the dire consequences that could befall those that did not keep the Sabbath holy, as we shall see on more than one occasion through this book. The church could also fulfil a role in terms of education, particularly because schooling was somewhat more basic in centuries past, and many people began work at a very early age rather than staying in learning environments. Many people grew up unable to read and write, and so learning had to take place in other ways.

The vicar's sermon would often be a key part of this in more recent history. However, in the medieval period, services would be held in Latin, meaning that many of the congregants did not understand what was being said. To help with this, churches at the time were often highly decorated with paintings depicting religious scenes. Many of these were lost during both the Reformation and the Victorian Restoration period—a time when the word "restoration" took on quite a different meaning to today.

Doom paintings were designed to highlight the differences between the rewards that would be found in Heaven for living a good life under the Church's direction and the terrors that awaited in Hell for anyone who strayed from that path. Whilst many of these paintings were quite crudely fashioned in smaller churches, there were some fine examples, of which the best-known is Michelangelo's "Last Judgment" in the Sistine Chapel. One of the best examples in Britain was rediscovered under whitewash in 1819 at the Church of St Thomas a Becket in Salisbury.

A story at Auxerre Abbey in France tells how the Devil was particularly unhappy about the way that he had been depicted in a wall painting there. A set of images had been created by a monk who had newly joined the abbey on a patch of wall that had remained bare, as none of the other brothers had the necessary skills to decorate it.

The images of Christ, Mary, and the joys found in Heaven were beautiful, but when it came to the depiction of the Devil, the monk did not hold back in the depiction of his hideous nature. One day, a mysterious stranger appeared at the abbey and suggested to the monk that he had ruined an otherwise delightful painting with something so ugly, and that he should consider making the Devil a more handsome character. The monk, who was up a ladder working on a high part of the painting at the time, called down to say that he was quite happy with the image as it was. The man became angry at this response and revealed his true form to the monk. Surprise, surprise! It was the Devil himself—who would have guessed it?! The Devil, according to the story, toppled the monk from his position up the ladder, but the holy man was saved by the intervention of the Virgin Mary. The method of this intervention was not recorded, so we, sadly, do not know whether she levitated him, appeared and caught him, or perhaps popped a small trampoline at the bottom of the ladder. Let's assume it was the latter.

The ringing of church bells, a quintessential sound which is part of everyday life for those of us who live in the country in particular, plays both a spiritual and a community role in the church. Campanology itself brings people together in a social group and ensures the traditions associated with church bells. The act of ringing them has many roles within the life of the church, and, hence, much folklore and superstition has grown up around it. The bells in many churches are hundreds of years old and are rung as a call to worship or in connection with weddings, funerals, and other notable events.

English poet John Donne's words "send not to know for whom the bell tolls. It tolls for thee" highlight the connection between bells and the funeral. Typically, a single bell is used, and the bell—as in Donne's words—is tolled, meaning that it is rung without the aperture of the bell being raised to the sky; a process known in bellringing as being "rung up."

Historically, prior to the funeral toll, there would have been two other occasions connected with a death where a church bell would be rung. The "passing bell" was rung approximately at the point of death in order to protect the soul from the Devil or other evil. Immediately after passing, the "death knell" would be rung. Later, royal statutes provided some regulation over these processes. This meant that ringing other than at the funeral would become gradually less common. The death knell, for example, could be sounded at the point at which the parish clerk was informed of a death. However, if this took place after sunset, then the tolling would be held over to the following morning in order to not disturb the nighttime peace of the community.

A few hundred years ago, a hand bell would sometimes be used instead of the church bell for tolling the passing bell. The church sexton would walk around the community, pausing periodically to ring the bell, announce the details of the death, and provide details about when and where the burial would take place. This proclamation would often be made in front of the houses of those who had known the deceased personally. When the day of the funeral arrived, the sexton would, again, ring the same bell, this time walking in front of the funeral procession.

Church bells were considered to be sacred, holy objects. When new bells were installed in a church, they would be anointed with oil in the same way as a human baptism. This was done to ensure that the Devil would be driven away whenever the bells were rung, and we can see how this feeds into the folklore connected with both the Devil and fairies fearing the sound of church bells.

This anointing meant that church bells were able to act in other positive ways as well. They could cure disease, purify the environment, and were even believed to ease labour pains during childbirth. This became a service, and women could pay for the church bells to be rung to help them have a birth that was as quick and pain-free as possible. Since this excluded the poorer members of the community, they would take to wrapping their girdle around the bell first, before wearing it as an act of power transference.

In some respects, we might consider church bells as being imbued with human traits, or, even in some extreme cases, almost anthropomorphic. Traditions arose in medieval times for punishing bells that had "sinned" somehow. If a bell fell from its tower and killed somebody, it would be taken down and stood upside down in the church, where it would be filled with thistles and thorn branches. The bell would remain here for seven years before it was considered to have been sufficiently punished, after which time it was reinstated.

It was in historic Russia that bells were seen as being especially human in nature. They had souls and their components were named after parts of the body. In 1591, following thc murder of Ivan the Terrible's youngest son, a bell was rung in alarm that incited a mass riot. The 320-kilogram bell was taken to the town square and a blacksmith was called to tear out its "tongue" (also known as "the clapper"). Following this, it was whipped a dozen times and finally dragged to Siberia where it was exiled in Tobolsk. The process took around a year to complete.

All sinners must be punished, of course, not just naughty bells. Sitting at the centre of the village community, the church also held this role as the location for the undertaking of punishment for minor offences. Both the village stocks and the whipping post were usually erected next to the churchyard, often on an adjacent village green. On occasion, they would be stored under the church tower when they were not being used.

The 1351 English Statute of Labourers Act required every town and village to own a set of stocks. The stocks are a wooden device designed to restrain an offender by the feet. Many people confuse these with the standing restraint which holds people by the hands and head, known as the *pillory.* The Statute of Labourers Act was not repealed until 1863, and the last recorded use of the stocks was not until 1872. In fact, their use has never been abolished in law.

The 1351 act cites the use of the stocks as being for "unruly artisans," and those confined would often be insulted, kicked, or spat at. In colonial America, stocks were used to hold prisoners awaiting trial, as well as for punishing those found guilty, and they were particularly favoured by Puritans who viewed them as being suitable for anyone of a lower rank than themselves.

The role of the church in any community should be as a safe and welcoming space for anyone. Despite what history's many holy wars may suggest, the church should be inclusive. In the Middle Ages, the ability to "seek sanctuary" in a holy place was written into law. Not only did this give a place for people to find shelter, but it would also prevent criminals from being arrested if they made it into the church before the law caught up with them. Nowadays, there is no such legal protection, but the church should still be viewed as a space where sanctuary could be found—at the very least metaphorically.

Nowhere, perhaps, is the role of the church as an inclusive space for all demonstrated more meaningfully than in the Black Church in America. An article from *The Harvard Gazette* excerpting from and discussing a book by Henry Louis Gates Jr. on the Black Church highlights this admirably:

> *We have to give the church its due as a source of our ancestors' unfathomable resiliency and perhaps the first formalized site for the collective fashioning and development of so many African American aesthetic forms. Although Black people made spaces for secular expression, only the church afforded room for it all to be practiced at the same time. And only in the church could all of the arts emerge, be on display, practiced and perfected, and expressed at one time and in one place … We do the church a great disservice if we fail to recognize that it was the first formalised site within African American culture perhaps not exclusively for the fashioning of the Black aesthetic, but certainly for its performance, service to service, week by week, Sunday to Sunday.*

We finally move outside of the church building and to the churchyard as the final resting place of many in a community. For a long time, the churchyard was the only available place of interment for most people. Some of the most wealthy and prominent members of society would find a burial spot inside the church, but these were unusual. There is a belief held by many that the smell from these internal graves is what led to the phrase "stinking rich." I have heard this also applied to the grand mausoleums found in some churchyards, but there is no evidence to substantiate this claim at all. The earliest printed reference to "stinking rich" comes from a Montana-based newspaper in the 1920s, where the prefix is used as a way of describing a large amount of wealth, much like "filthy rich."

Burial practices in churchyards have evolved significantly over time. High mortality rates in a larger population after the Industrial Revolution meant that there was high demand for gravesites, and individual plots were rare at this time. Churchyards became unsanitary places and, even into the early part of the nineteenth century, coffins might be placed a dozen or more deep in a grave, stacked with nothing to separate them. The coffins themselves were cheaply made and would even occasionally collapse before they had even been fully lowered into the ground. Even when in the ground, bodies would not find rest for long, as they were frequently dug up again after a short passing of time in order to free space for others. The corpses would then be burned.

To combat this problem, particularly in an urban environment, the Victorians developed the idea of the separate greenfield cemetery, often taking the form of a public park with footpaths to walk under a canopy of trees, with individual graves scattered amongst the bushes and flowers. This provided not only a pleasant final resting place for the dead, but also a better spot for those remaining to sit and contemplate the lives of their relatives.

Traditionally, the graves in a churchyard would face east, not only reflecting the Jewish practice of placing the dead to face the rising sun, but also in readiness for the Day of Judgment, when the Lord would, as described in the Bible, come from the east. The majority of burials would be placed on the south side of the church, with the ground to the north being used for the unbaptised, criminals, or those who took their own life. The exception to this was the vicars themselves, who were often buried with their feet facing the church, showing that they were still attendant to the needs of their parishioners.

It is usual for bodies to be buried in repose. Some standing burials are known in folklore, and, certainly, there is plenty of evidence for upright burial culturally throughout history. The Peruvians buried their royalty in this fashion. In China, upright burial has been suggested by the government more than once as a solution to the decreasing availability of land for the dead. Many cultures buried fallen warriors in an upright position as a mark of respect. In the Old Burying Ground at Beaufort in North Carolina, local folklore tells us that such a grave exists. This is said to belong to an unnamed British officer who died aboard a ship nearby at some point in the eighteenth century. He was buried in full dress uniform in a standing position, facing England and saluting the King.

Also buried in this graveyard around the same time is the body of a young girl who died at sea whilst travelling with her father. She had wanted to visit Europe, where her ancestors had lived, but her mother had not wanted her to take such a perilous voyage. Her father had accompanied her on the trip to keep her safe and make sure she returned home. He could not face the thought of her being buried at sea, so he bought a barrel of rum and preserved her body for the rest of the trip until they were able to make it to land back home. Her story has been so moving to many visitors that a tradition has arisen of leaving small toys on her grave as a mark of respect. This is a custom that is found on many graves with similarly tragic stories attached to them, as we shall see again in the next chapter.

St Anne's Limehouse Church on the fringes of London is home to a very unusual gravestone from the 1760s. It is inscribed on both sides, with one side being upside down. The history of this headstone is not known. Both sides are dedicated to the same burial, so it has not been repurposed in this way. However, perhaps the stonemason was not happy with the results first time around, but was also reluctant to completely scrap the stone.

The church itself is particularly interesting, being full of unusual features. There are often many secret, inaccessible rooms and chambers, a crypt that is so large that it was used in the Second World War as an air raid shelter, and a window with glass that is enamelled instead of the traditional staining process. However, the most well-known oddity here is an eight-foot stone pyramid in the churchyard.

The architect of the church, Nicholas Hawksmoor, is known to have been a freemason, and it is undoubtedly this fact that has led to it being connected with his interest in the occult. A figure of a unicorn is inscribed into the stone, as well as the words "wisdom of Solomon" both in English and in Hebrew. One theory put forward, which would not be out of place in a Dan Brown novel, is that the pyramid is one part of a bigger map of masonic and sacred symbols which Hawksmoor placed in various locations around this part of London, possibly as part of some Egyptian hieroglyphic connection. A void which exists beneath the pyramid lends itself to speculation as to what might be hidden underneath. In fact, the writer, Sax Rohmer, creator of Fu Manchu, located the character's opium den here.

The most probable truth behind the stone pyramid is somewhat more ordinary. It is likely that this is one of a pair of pyramids that were destined for the tops of the eastern towers of the church, but, at some point, the second one either became damaged or otherwise never made it to the church for some reason. The unused structure remains in situ to this day.

Nineteenth-century reports suggest that St Anne's Church is haunted by a ghost which is heard to have laughing fits in the middle of the night. With this dramatic and unnerving image in mind, we move on to explore the subject of spectral apparitions at the church and churchyard in more detail.

CHAPTER TWO

SPECTRAL FIGURES IN THE CHURCHYARD

AT FIRST GLANCE, the idea of ghosts in the church seems about as likely as *Snakes on a Plane.* If the church and its burial space is hallowed ground, then it should be under the protection of God and, therefore, does not seem the sort of place that ghosts would choose to hang around post-mortem. But there are plenty of reports of spectral figures on church ground, and plenty of folklore surrounding their meaning. So...chapter justified!

We need to pause for just a moment here and ask a difficult question. What are we talking about? What is a ghost?

To answer that in great detail and unpick the theology and philosophy behind it would need another book in itself, and even that would only scratch the surface. What we need to do here is to remember that we are approaching all of the topics in this book from the perspective of folklore. And, provided you started reading this book at the beginning, you should know roughly what this means.

For the folklorist, ghosts are found in the broader category of the *supernatural,* which in turn sits underneath the umbrella term of "belief." In folklore, a ghost is not a "thing," but is rather a concept. Different people will believe different things about the concept of a ghost. Some will see it as the spirit of a deceased person. Others may take the historical time slip approach. Others still may not believe in the idea of spectral apparitions at all. But even then, these people cannot deny that there are plenty of experiential reports from those who do. Therefore, the stories of such apparitions hold meaning—or held meaning—for those who witnessed or recorded them.

As far as the Church as an organisation goes, there is no firm answer to the ghostly question. The Catholic Church has attested to the voracity of a number of appearances of deceased saints. All Christian denominations believe in other spiritual beings such as angels or the souls of the dead. We can find references to ghosts in the Bible itself. In the first book of Samuel, the witch of Endor (referred to in many translations as a medium) conjures the ghost of the dead prophet at the insistence of Saul, who assures her that the Lord will not punish her for doing so.

> *"Then the woman asked, 'Whom shall I bring up for you?'*
> *'Bring up Samuel,' he said.*
> *When the woman saw Samuel, she cried out at the top of her voice and said to Saul, 'Why have you deceived me? You are Saul!'*
> *The king said to her, 'Don't be afraid. What do you see?'*
> *The woman said, 'I see a ghostly figure coming up out of the earth.'*
> *'What does he look like?' he asked.*
> *'An old man wearing a robe is coming up,' she said.*
> *Then Saul knew it was Samuel, and he bowed down and prostrated himself with his face to the ground.*
> *Samuel said to Saul, 'Why have you disturbed me by bringing me up?'"*[1]

1 1 Samuel 28:11–15.

On the resurrection of Christ, Matthew records in his gospel that the disciples first think that Jesus is a ghost until he informs them otherwise. This suggests that, although Christ is not a ghost, the concept of what a ghost was must have been known at that time and was recorded in Christian sacred text as such.

Some in the Church would discount these and other examples of spectral apparitions, instead ascribing them to demons manifesting and trying to trick the living. This in itself feeds into the idea within folklore of the replacement of motifs over time. For example, in texts from medieval England, people were afraid of *revenants*—creatures which would emerge from their grave at night spreading disease and death as they roamed. In later times, the ghost had replaced the undead as the source of the fear. However, beliefs in the destructive elements continued along similar lines.

Science cannot definitively prove or disprove the existence of ghosts, whatever they may be. And folklore doesn't seek to. With that in mind, we are in the best position to examine some of the ways in which spectral apparitions have been recorded on hallowed ground, and what their meaning might be.

One of the older types of spectral apparition which may be associated with hallowed ground is that of the church grim. This is a spirit which is said to guard the church from incursion of either supernatural origin or those in the mortal world who may want to cause harm, such as thieves or vandals. Unique to the folklore of England and that of Scandinavian countries, the church grim appears in animal form. Horses, rams, and a variety of birds including ravens have all been recorded as examples of church grims, but the most common motif found in folklore is that of a large black dog.

Spectral black dogs have been reported in the folkloric record all over the world since the twelfth century, but the United Kingdom is the richest area for cases that we might examine. It comes as no surprise to find the ghostly black dog acting as a church grim in this way. The creature may act both as a protector and guardian, or as an aggressor or portent in terms of its folklore. A flesh-and-blood dog serves both purposes depending on your viewpoint. If you an owner being threatened, then an animal protecting you is most definitely a "good dog." The attacker may see things from a different perspective. So it is with the church grim; it protects the churchyard, but those with sacrilege in mind will see it another way.

In Nordic lore, the guardian is known as a *Kirkegrim*, *Kyrkogrim*, or *Kirkonväki* in Denmark, Sweden, and Finland, respectively. In Scotland and a diminishing number of northern areas of the United Kingdom, the church grim may similarly be named *Kirk grim.* "Kirk" is a Scots and (no longer extant) northern English word which simply means *church.* In the United Kingdom outside of Scotland, it has died out other than in some dialects but survived in the Scots language probably because of its usage to refer to the national Church of Scotland.

Where the word "church" has Old English etymology, *kirk* is loaned from the Old Norse. Both words are related and may share the same root back in Greek origins.

The word grim is just one of a wide number of regional terms used to describe spectral black dogs. Outside of its association with church grim terminology, the word is used as a descriptor in the county of Lancashire, along with *Gytrash*, *Padfoot,* and some other minor terms. Most likely, as a county in the northwest of England, the term has remained in use as a remnant of the old church association.

Folklorists in the nineteenth century speculated that the church grim has its origins in the practice of burying an animal as a sacrifice in the foundations when raising a new building, based in the old belief that a structure built on blood will be the stronger. The idea is plausible, but we should not be too quick to accept some of these older claims of longevity without more evidence to back them up. Antiquarians of the period were very quick to find Druidic and Pagan roots in many folkloric practices, often when there were none to be found.

There is no disputing that foundation sacrifices took place, as we can find evidence for them all over the world, but making the tie to the church grim is much more difficult. There appear to be no—or possibly very scant—records of animals' bones interred in any churches in Britain, or at least those which suggest a sacrificial origin, but there are plenty of church grim stories. A stronger link is probably to be found in the old belief that the first burial in a new churchyard would have a role watching over the rest of the dead and protecting the ground from incursion by the Devil or other malicious forces. It is said that in order to prevent any deceased parishioner from having this arduous task, an animal would be interred first instead. A dog would be the most natural protector.

In volume two of his 1851 trilogy of books, *Northern Mythology*, for example, compiler Benjamin Thorpe presents a story relating to a battle between a Danish Kirkegrim and a Strand-varsel. *Strand-varsler* (plural) are the spirits of those who died at sea and whose bodies are washed up onto shore where the ground was not consecrated. Swedish folklore scholar Tommy Kuusela notes that in Sweden the word is *strandvaskare* and refers to the washing up of the body. The word *varsel,* in both Swedish and Danish, relates to an omen or portent, and so is probably a mistranslation in this case. The folkloric belief is that the spirit returns as a revenant, sometimes called a *strandgast,* and a similar motif is found in Norway in the form of the *draug,* named from the Old Norse *draugr.*

It was believed that these undead would try to make their way to hallowed ground where they could rest. The book records:

> *One night as a peasant was going along the strand towards Taarbek, a Strand-varsel sprang suddenly on his back and there clung fast, crying "Carry me to the church!" The man having no alternative, carried him the shortest way to Gientofte. On their reaching that village, and when close under the churchyard wall, the Varsel sprang quickly over it, when instantly the*

> *Kirkegrim approached, and an obstinate battle ensued between them. After having fought for a while, they both sat down to rest, when the Varsel said to the peasant: "Did I stand up well?" The peasant answered: "No." The battle then commenced anew, and when they again sat down to rest the Varsel again asked: 'Did I stand up well now?" and the peasant a second time answered: "No." The fight then recommenced, and the Varsel for the third time said: "Now! Have I stood up well?" and on the peasant answering: 'Yes." "It is well for thee," said the Varsel, "that thou hast answered so, for otherwise I would surely have broken thy neck."*

A similar, although folklorically slightly tangential, belief regarding the danger of being the first body to be buried in a churchyard centres around the idea that, rather than having to act as a guardian, the first interment would be claimed by the Devil. We can see the similarities between these stories and those regarding the building of new bridges, for example, where often a dog is driven over the bridge before it is used by humans for the same purpose. In the case of new churchyards, the folklore where it is related to the Devil more commonly leads to the burial of a person not connected with the parish rather than an animal. In one example from the north of England, for instance, the body of a sex worker is found in the street and buried. At St John's Church at Bovey Tracey in South Devon, it was said that the body of a servant of a visitor to the area was used for the same purpose.

In most English churches, or those that follow an English pattern of design, the division between the consecrated ground of the churchyard and the unconsecrated soil outside would lie underneath the lychgate.

The word *lych* remains unchanged from the original Old English and means "corpse." Many years ago, before the benefits of modern transportation, the bodies of anyone who died and lived a distance from their parish church would be carried along a dedicated path known as a "lychway"—sometimes today called a "corpse road." These journeys would often be many miles, and you can still find large flat stones in the landscape adjacent to lychways. These are now known as "coffin stones" and would have been used as a place to rest the body while taking a rest from walking.

The name is something of a misnomer, as most families would have been too poor to afford any form of coffin, so the body would therefore have just been wrapped in a shroud or winding sheet—the probable origin, incidentally, of the white-sheet ghost motif.

On entering through the wooden church gate, the funeral party would find themselves underneath the lychgate. This was a wooden structure not unlike a porch, with a sloped roof of thatch or tile. Beneath would be seats of stone or wood and a slab upon which they placed the body. It could be hours, or even days, between the arrival at the church and a vicar being ready to conduct the funeral service. The lychgate would provide shelter from the elements and allow a rotation of people to keep vigil over the body until burial to ensure that it did not become prey to body snatchers.

The Reverend Thomas Firminger Thistleton-Dyer collected much folklore, publishing a number of titles in the nineteenth century. He records a belief in England at one time that a person buried in the churchyard would then stand guard at the lychgate until the next interment, whose spirit would then take over the post. Possibly, this was recorded at churches where there was no legend of a church grim. The same belief was found in Scotland, where this supernatural watch over the church and its graveyard was known as the *faire chlaidh*.

This "rota" of protection appears to share the burden of protection, rather than it being the sole job of one spirit as we see with the grim.

As a boundary between the churchyard and the land outside, the lychgate forms one of those liminal in-between spaces which are so important in folklore; therefore, it is no surprise to find such beliefs attached to it. Not all of these were related to death, either. There is contradictory folklore surrounding the lychgate and marriages, for example. Sometimes, this was a spot at which children would form a barrier to exit for the bride and groom after the ceremony, sometimes with a garland or similar. The happy couple would have to pay a small tithe to pass through the gate and receive good luck. But in other churches, it was seen to invite ill-fortune at a wedding for the lychgate to be used. The church at Kneesall in Derbyshire, for instance, was said to have two gates, with the second being known as the "bride gate."

A slate gravestone set into the wall of the lychgate at the church of St Clement, near Truro in Cornwall, appears to have a ghost story attached to it, which has remarkable similarities to other folklore. It is inscribed with the name of Betsey, a girl who appears to have died just before reaching her twentieth year in the last decade of the eighteenth century. Despite there being little known about the girl or the true reason for her passing, flowers seem to be placed on the top of the stone every year to mark the anniversary of the date she died.

Betsey Tregaskis was the daughter of parents William and Elizabeth, who ran the inn at St Clement. Long since closed, this was located adjacent to the church in the centre of three terraced, thatched cottages, which still remain just a few yards from the churchyard. There is more than one version of the circumstances surrounding her death.

Descendants of the Tregaskis family state that Betsey died of tuberculosis, a bacterial disease of the lungs which, although highly treatable today, was historically responsible for the deaths of many, being also known as consumption or the "white death." Folklore, however, suggests that Betsey took her own life after falling pregnant with a gentleman of a class much above her own.

The inter-class pregnancy is a particularly well-worn trope and accounts for a number of hauntings, as well as quite a few stories about the deaths of unwanted babies, most of which have no historical basis to them. Interestingly, just over the border in Devon, the well-known roadside grave attributed to Kitty Jay is said to be the final resting place of a servant girl who took her life after suffering a similar fate. Here as well, fresh flowers have always been mysteriously found on the grave, only this time they appear year-round.

It seems likely that Betsey's headstone has been relocated to the interior of the lychgate to preserve it, having probably once been in the churchyard but possibly having fallen or been moved if the grave was reused. It is not, in fact, the only stone set into the lychgate wall. The fact that suicides were not permitted to be buried in consecrated ground feeds nicely into the idea that the liminal spot of the lychgate allows for the body to be placed as closely as possible. There are similar folk stories about the bodies of wicked men who were refused burial in consecrated ground being placed inside the wall of the church, for example, providing a neat loophole to the problem.

Whatever the true reason for Betsey's death, it has apparently not stopped her ghost from appearing in the area. An author who lives in the same terrace of cottages that used to house the Tregaskis's inn recalled that a coach party who visited the church once enquired as to whether there was an historic reenactment taking place. There wasn't, but it turned out that they had seen a girl who they described as wearing old-fashioned dress and a mob cap.

Although the description is somewhat vague, this story is not without its curiosity. As an item of clothing, the mob cap was mostly the reserve of higher classes in the Georgian period. The cap part was linen and worn indoors, and then underneath was simply known as a bonnet. This consisted of a caul and a frilled brim, often with a ribbon band. It was essentially a fashion item in the eighteenth century when country clothing was in vogue. The name "mob cap," in fact, comes from the French Revolution, where the rioting women wore them. By the Victorian period, the caps were no longer seen as fashionable but were retained as headgear by girls working in the service industry. This is the stereotype which seems more likely to be what was reported, but it does not fit the time period of Betsey's death.

The trope of forbidden love spanning classes is not just confined to the United Kingdom. A story not unlike that of Betsey Tregaskis, Kitty Jay, and many others may be found in South Carolina, with only the pregnancy being absent and the classes of the two involved reversed.

Some claim to have sighted the ghost of a girl in the graveyard of All Saint's Church in Pawleys Island, clasping her hand to her chest and looking as if she is searching for something. She is believed to be Alice Flagg, a girl from a nineteenth-century upper-class South Carolina family who fell in love with a man below her perceived station. The two became engaged secretly, defying the instruction of her brother who forbade the match.

In order to keep their partnership concealed, Alice wore her ring on a ribbon, but they were still found out and Alice was despatched to boarding school in Charleston, where she stayed until she became very ill and was taken back to her family. As her condition worsened, her brother discovered the ring, tore it from her neck, and threw it away. Alice never recovered.

It is a very common idea that the spirits of those who pass away with some kind of unfinished business in life will not rest until they have seen it concluded, and this would certainly apply to Alice. She has been sighted both in the graveyard and also at the family home, and in both locations, she can be seen with her hand held to the position where the ring would have hung. Like the previous stories, her grave also sees an accumulation of flowers and other small items. In this case, they are brought by many visitors, either as a mark of respect or to try and make contact with her spirit. In much the same way that the folklore spread around more well-known gravesites, such as that of Mercy Brown, superstition has developed around the Flagg grave. It is said that if you walk around it in the right combination of circuits and leave a token, she will grant your wish. We will examine superstitions in churches and churchyards in more detail in the final chapter of the book.

Sometimes, the stories of ghosts that inhabit our churchyards come about because the graves in which the mortal remains were buried are of a particularly unusual design. In the same way that glacial erratics (stones made of different material from the normal geology of an area, deposited there in the ice age by glacial flow) are often associated with giants or the Devil throwing them, it is natural for a tomb or monument that stands out from the rest to have folk tales grow around it.

In the graveyard of Holy Trinity Church, Buckfastleigh, stands a rare example of a "penthouse tomb" —one of only a small number surviving in the United Kingdom. Square in shape with a pointed roof, a wide iron grille is set into the wall facing the south door of the church with a lockable wooden door in the wall opposite. Contained within this structure is an altar tomb, which contains the remains of various members of the Cabell family, wealthy local landowners who held a manor house named Brook in the area.

This unusual tomb has, for many years, been the focus of a number of superstitious stories and ghostly legends, in part connected with its design. It used to be said by local children that if you walked around the tomb a certain (and variable) number of times and then put your finger into the keyhole of the door, the devil would appear and bite your fingertip. Local mythology also told how Squire Richard Cabell was such a wicked character that he was buried in this prison-like tomb, with the further addition of a large stone placed on his head so that his spirit would not rise again and trouble the living any further. The character is probably one of a number who served as inspiration to Sir Arthur Conan Doyle when writing *The Hound of the Baskervilles* due to the suggestion that Cabell was either hunted to his death by spectral black dogs, or that the same creatures were baying at the window as he lay on his deathbed.

In actuality, there is a complex history of the Cabell family to unpack in order to understand exactly how these stories may have originated. There were three different Richard Cabells, the first of which was buried in the tomb alongside the remains of his wife Suzannah in 1613. At this point, only the tomb itself was in place, with the penthouse constructed later. The second Richard had some disagreements in the town but nothing to warrant the legendary reputation, and the third was disliked because of his wealth and character but, again, not to the extent that the stories suggest. It is probable that an amalgamation of facts, and a certain amount of fiction, led the story to develop in the way that it did.

Some similar elements can be found in a grave said to be cursed, found on the Rothiemurchus Estate in Strathspey, near Aviemore in the Cairngorms area of Scotland. Taking its name from the hill above it, the Doune is a seventeenth century mansion house belonging to the Grant family, who have been associated with the estate for over four hundred years. An old parish church, with the associated graveyard, forms part of the Rothiemurchus Estate.

Before it passed to the Grants, the Estate was in the hands of the Shaw family, and the grave in question is that of the clan chief known as "The Great Shaw," Seath Mór Sgorfhiaclach or, more commonly, Farquhar Shaw. Known as a great warrior, "The Great Shaw" commanded the Clan Chattan in the Battle of the Clans at Perth in 1396. He is said to be the only man who survived, and the gravestone records him as "Victor in the Combat at Perth."

Farquhar Shaw died and was buried in 1405, and the grave is linked with a number of ghostly sightings as well as being said to have an elf-like spirit guardian. On top of the gravestone are five stones, each about nine inches in diameter. It is these that are supposed to be cursed, bringing misfortune or far worse to those who interfere with them. The stones appear to have a curious habit of finding their way back to the place that they came from should they be moved.

Two other similarly shaped stones in the same graveyard mark the final resting places of two footmen, both of whom suffered the same fate at different times. Robert Scroggie, footman to the Duchess of Bedford, was accidentally drowned whilst bathing in the local river in 1830. Robert Latham, footman to the Marchioness of Abercorn, also drowned in the same river seven years later. Both were in their early twenties.

The local belief was that both men had died because they had interfered with the stones on Farquhar Shaw's grave. Scroggie was said to have carried one of them to the river and thrown it in a week before he died, although the stone was miraculously back in its normal resting place by the following morning.

A journalist in the 1940s was said to have tried lifting one of the stones on the grave above his head and died the following day in a car accident. A more modern case from 1978 was said to involve three friends. The first, and only one in the example to be named, was Leslie Walker. He touched one of the stones and then came down with a high fever which lasted for six weeks. The friend who then rearranged the stones died in the cemetery itself of a cerebral haemorrhage. The third, who had no direct involvement, was hospitalised with pains to the stomach.

Of course, over a period of many centuries, it is likely that many people will have touched the stones and suffered no ill effects at all. Reported stories where the curse came true provide the confirmation bias necessary to allow the legend to persist. At the same time, other stories provide no definite outcome whilst still enabling the story to persist. For example, an article in *Country Life*, dated 24 December 1948, notes:

> *About twenty years ago the Doune of Rothiemurchus was converted into a hotel. While I was staying there in 1935, one of the country people told me of a baker in the neighbourhood who, when a choir-boy at the old church of Rothiemurchus and in company with some other boys of his own age, took delight in removing these five stones from the recumbent slab upon which*

they may still be seen. This he did, as he maintained, in order to prove the absurdity of the belief that dire misfortune must necessarily overtake him who treats them contemptuously. Local history does not record whether the baker and his contemporaries ultimately suffered for their behaviour; but it does record that, although they often hid the stones in all manner of places—in rabbit-burrows, for instance—by some means unexplained, nay, inexplicable, they always found their way back to their age-old position in the kirkyard.

An iron grate was installed over the grave of Farquhar Shaw in 1983. Popular stories now suggest that this was done for "the safety of the public." What seems more likely is that it was done to stop legend-trippers from following in the footsteps of others and pilfering the stones. At the beginning of the same year, the *Aberdeen Evening Express* newspaper had already reported two instances from the previous twelve months of the stones having been taken. In the first, they were recovered in the same week, and in the second, nearly five months later.

Of the first case, the police apparently reported that they knew who the thief was and were able to declare that they were still in good health!

Interestingly, the grate that was installed is precisely the same design as the old mortsafes, which used to be placed over graves in order to prevent bodysnatchers from exhuming recently interred corpses. Thanks to the joys of social media, these are the photographs which are now constantly circulated by misinformed people as "anti-vampire devices."

Folklore often grows around characters in a community who stand out in particular ways: the intellectually advanced, those highly skilled in certain crafts, the wealthy and influential, or fierce warriors such as Shaw. We often see the supernatural being ascribed to such people. The blacksmith or weaver can only have received their skills from a bargain with the Devil. Often, those with wealth and status in a community abuse that power and so in death, their ghosts become malicious too. Sometimes the stories are conflated with other people like Richard Cabell, and sometimes the people genuinely deserve their fate.

In the village churchyard at Lapford, in mid Devon, lies the grave of a previous rector of the church, Reverend John Radford. Known locally as "Parson Jack," Radford was a notorious character once described as "as odd a specimen of a Christian minister as the Devil himself could ordain for the work." Local beliefs about Parson Jack in the nineteenth century included suspicions that he had gotten a servant girl pregnant, drowning her in the rectory pond when he discovered the fact, and that he had killed a curate who was deputising at the church.

These stories are unproven and may well be apocryphal based on the general dislike of Radford as a person. But what is certainly true is that he was once imprisoned in Exeter Jail for attacking a toll-collector on the road out of the city. As a vicar, the law exempted Radford from paying at toll gates when travelling, providing that he was on church business. The business for which Parson Jack normally travelled to Exeter, however, was that of drinking and street wrestling, both of which he was inordinately fond of. The altercation took place after a particular heavy session. The police were called after Radford pulled a knife on the pikeman (as the collectors at toll gates were known), but rather than submitting to them, Parson Jack was up for a fight. It took four gentlemen of the law to overpower him and cart him off to prison.

John Radford's body was interred in the churchyard in Lapford after his death in 1861, but not in the place that he had wanted to be buried. This itself has generated much folklore and some contradiction as to why it happened in the first place. It is said that Radford's wish was to be buried inside the chancel of the church, but his grave is to be found outside the north wall of the chancel. This is the area of the churchyard which used to be reserved for bodies who were unlikely to find salvation in the eyes of the church: the unbaptised, characters of ill-repute, and those who took their own life.

Most of the stories say that the villagers elected to bury Parson Jack in this position as revenge for his wicked character and deeds. But an opposing story suggests that the residents of Lapford did, in fact, try very hard to have him buried inside the chancel, but were opposed and ultimately overthrown in their efforts by the church authorities themselves.

Whichever is the reason, Parson Jack's spirit is naturally restless because of this. One result of this is that the grave is the most unstable one in the churchyard to this day. Due to its inability to remain vertical, the cross that makes up Radford's headstone had to be cemented into position and is now braced to the rear with a strip of metal.

Many people had reportedly sighted the ghost of Parson Jack Radford over the years, as his is said to be able to leave his resting place through a small hole about the size of an adult fingertip. His aim is to try and reach the Old Rectory, where he used to reside in life, but his spirit is bound to only be permitted to travel at the rate of one cockstride a year.

"Cockstride ghosts" are common in folklore and are usually associated either with characters who are meting out some penance for things they did in life, or those who were buried in the wrong place and have to return to where they should be. In this latter case, they are often making their way back to a churchyard from another position. Such is the case for the ghost of an unnamed woman at the village of Coffinswell, also in Devon. Her spirit was restless because she had been buried at the site of a local well rather than in the hallowed ground of the church. A ghost-laying parson (we will learn more about these in Chapter Five) from the local area granted her spectre permission to move from her current resting place to the churchyard, but only at the rate of one cockstride at midnight each New Year's Eve. Being a boundary not only between night and day, but also between years, this is a double-header for those who are fond of the liminal spaces in these stories!

A curious, and even more controversial, parallel with the story of Parson Jack Radford can be found in the reported hauntings at St Mary's Episcopal Church in Kansas City.

This church was first established in the area as St Luke's Mission in 1854. At this time, the congregation would gather at different places in the neighbourhood, but by 1867, the church was flourishing and had become able to purchase land, on which it built its first permanent church building.

At this point in history, the Kansas City area was in some flux, with the ministry of Catholic beliefs growing rapidly thanks the immigration of large numbers of Irish workers who were actively encouraged to travel and labour on the city's expansion. This had led to much protest and unrest from local groups fighting to "protect" American residents from the incursion of foreign Catholic rhetoric. It is a story which still, sadly, sounds very familiar to us in the twenty-first century.

It was against this uncertainty that a new priest was appointed to St Luke's mission in 1879. This rector, Henry D. Jardine, was one of a number of Protestant Episcopal clergymen at that time who supported a return to the old Anglo-Catholic ceremony of the church.

Jardine seems to have been a bit of a rebellious character in his youth, having been imprisoned for two years for his involvement in robbing his brother-in-law's factory business when he was just sixteen. It was during this jail term that he is said to have found his religious beliefs.

From the very beginning of his tenure as Rector, Henry Jardine's actions started to displease in the community. Dressed in the traditional full-length cassock of the Roman Catholic church, Jardine brought altar boys into the church, used candles and incense, and aimed for all the ritualism of a Catholic service. Alongside all of these difficulties, Jardine began to get something of a reputation for his dealings with the female congregants.

The local newspaper began to investigate the church—and the rector in particular—after two of its members were excommunicated for attending whilst drunk. A locally published pamphlet discussed this and Jardine's time of incarceration, and when the newspaper reprinted the pamphlet's contents, its owner found himself excommunicated too. This led to a further article in the paper a few days later which implied that some of the rector's private confessions were somewhat unusual. In one case, it was alleged that he had been found dishing out penance to a young lady using a slipper on her less-than-fully-clothed body.

Attempts were made to clear Jardine's name in court, but these cases all ended up being dismissed due to there being little evidence with which the priest's representatives could actually show that the charges were false.

Despite all of this, Father Jardine returned to church to preach, with both him and his assistants in the vestry wearing revolvers in case of any trouble. None was found there, but more difficulties did surface much later in the shape of an investigation by the ecclesiastical court. This found sufficient evidence to find Jardine guilty not only of acting inappropriately with female members of the church, but also of regular use of chloroform as a treatment for nerves.

After a failed attempt at a retrial was made, Jardine was found dead in somewhat suspicious circumstances in the sacristy of St Mary's Church just before the announcement of the ecclesiastical court's decision to remove him from service was made. Next to his body lay a bottle of chloroform, a handkerchief was on his face, and, most curiously, a rusty chain made of iron welded around his waist, much like the chains we might associate with the ghosts of the penitential deceased.

The Bishop of the Episcopal Church ruled the death of Henry D. Jardine as suicide, but the local medical examiner was not so certain, and the manner of death remains debatable. What was not up for discussion, of course, was the location at which the body might be interred. As the official ruling from the church was that Jardine took his own life, he could neither be buried in any consecrated place or in the foundations of the altar of a new church, as would have been the wishes of the church under other circumstances. He was buried in Elmwood Cemetery in Kansas City, but in 1921, his remains were finally moved to St Luke's Burial Ground, the consecrated space for all priests who served St Mary's Church.

As might be expected from a story of such controversies and scandal, there have many reports of sightings of Father Jardine's unquiet ghost. People alone in St Mary's Church at night have reported uncomfortable feelings, as if someone was watching them, and some of have smelt burning incense.

According to the archives of the episcopal church, organist Keith Gottschall was passing the building in the last decade of the twentieth century when he saw what seemed to be a figure floating by a window belonging to the music office on the second floor of the church. On entering the church and walking up to that area, it was found that the door was locked but noises could be heard from the room beyond. Gottschall experienced a cold space in the area that unnerved him, so he left for a short while. When he returned, the door was unlocked.

Before it was the music office, this area of the church had comprised the living quarters of the Reverend Edwin Merrill, who served St Mary's for over fifty years. He reported frequently hearing someone walking up the back stairs to this room at night when the building was empty, as well as noises from around the area of the high altar, which is dedicated to Henry Jardine.

In the year 2000, church members finally decided to move the remains of Father Jardine to this altar, where they would have normally been placed. Upon exhuming his grave at Forest Hill Cemetery, they found both his bones and a small box containing the iron chain. Both of these are now beneath the altar that has his dedication.

As you might expect, a story such as this has invited a certain amount of "ghost hunting" at the site. It is said that one person investigating with an electromagnetic field meter found high energy spikes both in the area of the music room and the altar. Photographs of the altar allegedly showed a figure looking like a priest carrying a candle. Research has found no trace of these images so far.

Other photographs of spectral figures in churches are much easier to come by, and a couple of them have achieved celebrity status over the years. Probably the most well-known of these is the image of an inexplicably tall, semi-transparent cowled figure with a white shrouded face, which is known colloquially as the Newby Monk.

The photograph was taken at the altar of the Church of Christ the Consoler, in the grounds of Newby Hall at Skelton-cum-Newby, North Yorkshire in 1963 by the Reverend Kenneth F. Lord. The somewhat imposing Victorian Gothic Revivalist-styled church was designed by English architect William Burges from a commission in June 1870, with construction completed in 1876.

The Newby Monk is arguably the most well-known of all photographs of ghosts in churches. Its clarity, unusual proportions, and somewhat creepy face all help to cement this claim, along with the fact that it was featured in the now-iconic 1970s Usborne children's book on ghosts from its *Mysteries of the Unexplained* series. The fact that it was taken by a vicar, who declared that there had been nothing visible at the time that the photograph was taken, adds a little voracity in itself.

Photographs claimed to be ghosts are naturally as divisive as anything else in the supernatural sphere, and there will always be a split between believers and those who are more sceptical. Despite being just over six decades old now, opinion is still very firmly divided on the Newby Monk image. Some have levelled the argument that the photograph appears to be somewhat staged, but if the original intention of the vicar was to take a photograph of the ornate altar in all its finery, then some care would have been taken to frame the image in the first place, so this argument probably holds little water.

There are a couple of interesting notable points about the image itself. It is often shown in a cropped format in order to foreground the ghostly image a little more. Two problems arise from doing this. One is that it loses the original framing intention, which adds an element of mistrust because the image then looks like it is focussing on the one area for no particular reason. Cropping also removes the bottom of the image of the ghost, which destroys any kind of height reference.

It has been calculated by some that the figure would have to stand at a height approaching nine feet when looking at the original uncropped version of the photograph. Fortunately, modern images of the altar show that it is very much unchanged from the 1960s; even the same altar cloth is in place today. This removes any speculation on this point. Whilst it is true that the figure would have to be unnaturally tall, you can see from the original image that the robes meet the floor and so, if fakery were involved, it would be very easy for a human figure to be standing on a box or small riser in order to create this effect.

Claims have been made that the ghost resembles that of a monk as they would look in the sixteenth century, possibly wearing a shroud or other facial covering to mask a disease such as leprosy. This immediately raises a couple of questions. Firstly, why would it appear at this altar when the church was not founded until the nineteenth century? And secondly, if ghosts are generally understood to be the post-mortem spirits of people who were once living, does this mean that monks in the sixteenth century were nine feet tall?

The photograph has been examined many times, twice by teams of experts working on behalf of television documentaries. Even here, the opinion was split. A team working for the BBC in the 1980s, examining a number of supernatural photographs, decided that the image was not a double-exposure and that computer technology, which was advanced at that time, showed no evidence of manipulation. A decade later, according to an internet forum discussion post written in 2002, another expert working on behalf of the ITV programme *Strange But True?* analysed the Newby Monk photograph and found evidence that glints of light in the eye sockets of the shrouded face showed that whoever had been wearing the costume had also been wearing glasses underneath, and that the image was a double exposure. However, whilst the programme, first broadcast in 1992 as the first episode of the fourth season of the show, does show the image, it is never referred to in the commentary or analysed. So there seems to be little evidence that this analysis is in the public domain.

Interestingly, a white line along the altar cloth which appears to have been caused by some sort of scratch or cut appears in every reproduced version of this image, which means that it must have been present in the original film negative. Nobody knows what happened to this.

There have been many similar semi-transparent—though usually more human looking—spectral figures photographed in churches, although some are more-oft reproduced than others. As double exposure, whether intended or accidental, was not uncommon in older film cameras, this seems to be a likely explanation for most of them. Subsequent reproductions of the images and retellings of the stories can naturally cause more folklore to form around them.

A bank manager called Mr. Bootman photographed the interior of the church at Eastry, Kent, in 1956. His image seems to show the partly faded image of a figure sitting in the frontmost of the pews. Two curious points come up from this photograph. One is that, although the framing is quite pleasing, there is really nothing of note in the image; the font is in the far background, and there are no monuments or interesting features on the walls. Unless the photographer was a particular enthusiast for pews, which is possible, it seems more likely that the figure was intentionally the subject of the shot even through Mr. Bootman claimed that the only person in the church other than himself was a cleaning lady. The second point of note is that, although the figure is obviously wearing spectacles and a clerical collar contemporary with the time the image was taken, many of the later reproductions and discussions around the image have referred to the figure as a "phantom monk." As there is no good evidence for any monastery at Eastry, with the only claimed possibility being one founded by King Egbert in 673 and that being historically unlikely, these references to a monk only serve to reshape the narrative of the photograph further.

The parish church at Woodford in Northamptonshire probably stands on the site of an earlier place of religious worship, with the current structure having had its nave and chancel built in the twelfth century. A number of ghostly sightings in this building may stem from the discovery by Victorian workmen shoring up an archway in the nave of a concealed object in a stone recess. At the time, it did not appear to be anything extraordinary, and so they roughly removed it from the stonework, from where it fell to the ground and shattered. Examination showed that the object had been enclosed in a box made of bamboo, and that wrapped in cloth inside was a mummified human heart.

Although most of the box and some of the heart itself were in poor condition, the valves were perfectly preserved and still are, as the vicar of the time had the foresight to place the remains in a sealed glass box. These showed without doubt that the heart was human.

Legends grew up around the heart, suggesting that it might have belonged to a local Lord or to a knight fighting in the crusades. However, the later discovery and translation of a thirteenth century mortuary record written in Medieval Latin showed that when the body of one Robert de Kirkton was buried in Norfolk in 1280, his heart was removed and embalmed before being placed in Woodford Church. It is now back in the recess where it was originally found.

In 1966, two teenagers named David and Gordon spent their summer holidays exploring local villages and photographing them. They stopped off at the church at Woodford, where they took a photograph of the altar and church interior, which has joined the ranks of the well-circulated church ghost images. Their colour image appears to show a figure dressed in some sort of white robe with a belt, somewhat reminiscent of a medieval knight, kneeling at the altar. The image, as well as a newspaper clipping from the time reporting on it, are still displayed in the church today.

The two boys have always asserted that there was nobody in shot when the photograph was taken. The camera was on a tripod and the photo was taken with a two-second exposure time, which has all meant that meaningful attempts to recreate the image could be attempted, although these have had little success. Analysis of the image has been undertaken by the manufacturers of the original film stock, Agfa, and found no evidence of double exposure or fault in the materials. Other computer analysis has concluded that the image was not manipulated after it was taken, and that whatever is in frame must have been there at the time.

There has been no conclusive disproving of the Woodford image to date, with the most plausible explanation offered being that the figure is that of a cleaner kneeling to scrub the altar floor, with the photograph being an incomplete exposure and the photographers being mistaken, or choosing to not disclose, that there was somebody in the frame.

Not all ghosts, of course, are so usefully visible. Sometimes, experiences are less visual and involve the other senses instead, much like the sounds and smells in the Henry Jardine haunting. Such was the case at St Mary's Church in Avenbury, in the county of Herefordshire.

This church is a particularly interesting site, and one ideally placed for the generation of folklore. As a place of worship, St Mary's continued to serve rural farms and isolated homes in the area long after the village of Avenbury itself was abandoned in the first half of the nineteenth century. It finally ceased providing religious service in 1931 and fell into a state of ruin, although restoration work on the site is currently ongoing.

The last vicar to be incumbent at the site reported a number of strange auditory phenomena at the church, including hearing the bell ringing and the organ playing after the building had been closed up for the night. He was far from alone in this. Many people walking the footpath that runs close to the church ruins have heard organ music, even before happening upon the church. As far back as the 1880s, a couple out walking on Christmas Day who became caught in snow took shelter on the church porch. Whilst there, they heard sounds coming from inside the building despite, the door being locked. They described them as happy and joyous rather than feeling any sense of foreboding.

Not all of the vicars were as accepting of the phenomena. A decade before the closure of the church, the Reverend E. H. Archer-Shepherd wrote a letter to the local newspaper to deny that the site was haunted and that he personally laid a ghost with the aid of twelve lighted candles. The letter was published on 18 September 1919 and had come in response to stories about the haunted church bringing reporters from a number of national newspapers to cover the incidents.

The vicar addressed the stories of ghostly organ music in some detail, acknowledging that it had been heard by a number of people, often with multiple witnesses. He suggested that the first example was on 8 September 1896, by the wife of the previous vicar and their three adult children. Evidently Archer-Shepherd was not aware of the story of the walking couple in the porch when he first penned the letter, although he subsequently heard from the wife of the pair and told her story in a postscript.

"To work the pedals of an organ or harmonium," wrote the vicar, "and to press down the keys, would require the expenditure of a considerable amount of physical force, of which I cannot conceive the disembodied spirits of a mere man to be capable."

Reverend Archer-Shepherd preferred the theory that the cause of the music was some kind of mental response in those that heard it, caused by telepathy, auto-suggestion, or atmospheric causes.

History tells us that St Mary's has been connected to some other significant events which could have left their mark on the site, both folklorically and in terms of its potential for possible supernatural curiosity. Amongst the other stories associated with it are two which carry very strong folklore motifs. One is a story somewhat scant in detail, but certainly strong in lore.

It was said that a local woman was refused burial in the graveyard at St Mary's because she had the reputation of being an unpleasant character and was viewed as a witch. The curate of the church tried to act as a mediator to this problem and had the woman's body laid to rest in a place not too far away, past a bend in the River Frome, which flowed past the church. This, however, did not satisfy the people of the village, so they dug up the body and threw it into the river. Since then, sightings of shapes both by the river and in the ruins of the church have been attributed to the woman, although in the latter case there is no obvious reason as to why the random glowing shape should be her and not anybody else.

Another candidate would be the ghost of Nicholas Vaughan, a man who was said to have been responsible for burning down a house belonging to the Bishop of the area. Vaughan is something of a notorious surname in the area, as Sir Thomas Vaughan, a fifteenth-century squire with an evil reputation, had lived just twenty-five miles away at Hergest Court. Known as "Black Vaughan," he was said to have haunted the area in the form of a black bull, accompanied by the spirit of his bloodhound. Fear of this ghost was so strong that an exorcism was conducted to lay his spirit to rest, although the bloodhound remained long afterwards. Some suggest that Sir Thomas Vaughan was another one of the inspirations drawn on by Sir Arthur Conan Doyle when writing *The Hound of the Baskervilles,* as the Baskerville family occupied an adjoining estate.

The ghost of Nicholas Vaughan was certainly associated with the ground surrounding St Mary's Church, and much like Sir Thomas who had come before, his presence was enough to scare the locals into calling for an exorcism. Of course, the similarities between the two—close in terms of geography, although disparate in chronology—mean that we should have some caution surrounding the possibility of conflation between the two stories.

Regardless, this exorcism took the form of the local parson "reading down" the spirit and trapping it in a box. This container, with silver trim, was buried in the bed of the river underneath the bridge that led to the old village of Avenbury. Workers renovating this bridge in the 1980s allegedly rediscovered the box. They found it to be empty...or maybe they released Vaughan's spirit back the churchyard?

Whilst the sounds coming from St Mary's Church had no malice to them, in terms of folklore it is the case that more earth-bound noises can have more supernaturally detrimental results. The sounds of church bells ringing as a call to worship are a traditional and welcome part of a Sunday morning for many, but not the fairy folk, who are said to have a strong aversion to church bells. There are many examples in the folklore record of local fairies and pixies being driven off by the sound of church bells.

In Northumberland, though, it seems that the fairies suffered a much worse fate. In the grounds of Brinkburn Priory is a shady area said to be the burial spot of the Northumberland fairies. Probably the first mention of this area as a fairy graveyard is found in the 1846 *Local Historian's Table Book* by Moses Richardson, who eloquently notes that "truly a more suitable place could not have been devised as the scene of so purely poetic a belief."

The connection with the church bells is drawn by the Yorkshire tradesman and folklore collector Michael Aislabie Denham. Between 1846 and 1859, Denham published a series of fifty-four pamphlets of much of the folklore that he collected, which became known as the Denham Tracts. In these, he notes that the fairy graveyard at Brinkburn is the only example of the fairies being killed by church bells in this way.

The idea of the mortality of the fairies coming about because of the ringing of the church bells is undoubtedly a commentary on the death of fairy beliefs in the area—a move from the older superstitions to more enlightened thinking fuelled by the power of the Christian church. It is an idea that we find time and again in different areas of folklore. The fairy graveyard itself would most likely have been what we tend to now call a "fairy ring," a grassy area outlined with a circle of mushrooms. These rings occur as a result of a single fungus, growing under the surface of the earth, putting out small threads called *mycelium* which form the circular circumference. On an annual basis, these threads will put out individual mushrooms. Each year, as the underground fungus grows, the fairy ring will increase in size.

The well-known Shropshire folklorist Charlotte Sophia Burne noted that in the Market Drayton area, people would refuse to use parts of the graveyard where fairy rings were growing. The belief in the fairies, and associated fears of what they could do, would still have been strong at this time.

In Scandinavia, the fairy folk were made of stronger stuff, and the Nisse who lived in Besser Church, one of the oldest churches in the Samsoe area of Denmark, used to cause trouble for the sexton by tying rags around the clapper of the church bell to stop it from sounding.

Apparently, the church will not always win out, and sometimes the spectral forces at work will have the upper hand!

CHAPTER THREE

FLORA AND FAUNA

"How fragile so-ever the sapling may be,
'Tis doomed to shaking ere it grows to tree.
At present 'tis not so much that is seen
Of this sombre old tree, which stands between
The past and the present, the old and the new,
That I am concerned with and telling to you
But rather 'tis this the truth I'm revealing,
The Yew is healer, its powers of healing
Surpasses the body, it extends to the soul!
Poor and dejected, wilt thou be made whole
Why should you suffer such anguish of mind,
And ever be seeking for what you can't find
Drugs and potations, all fail to control
Those greatest afflictions, those ills of the soul.
Turn thy sad soul to this grand old tree
Be earnest, be faithful, and thou shalt be free."

THESE WORDS ARE FROM the latter half of a poem penned and published in 1906 by Charubel, the pseudonym of the Welsh mystic John Thomas. Whereas many Welsh writers who adopted

Bardic names were antiquarians and members of the clergy, Thomas had eschewed his early study for entry into the Christian ministry to follow more occult interests, acting as a curative *Mesmerist.* Mesmerism was the theory, advanced by German doctor Franz Mesmer, that all living creatures had a natural force which could be harnessed, often through magnetism, for healing.

In this poem, however, from his 1906 book *The Psychology of Botany, Minerals and Precious Stones,* he is speaking of the most quintessential of all churchyard fauna, the yew tree. He refers to the churchyard yew in something of a liminal way, standing on the threshold between the "past and the present, the old and the new." Indeed, the yew was often found on the boundary between the consecrated ground of the churchyard and the lands beyond.

Much has been written of the yew, but not all of its history and meaning that has been widely published is necessarily accurate, so let's try and unpick the lore and lay down the facts, as well as the beliefs, in a meaningful way.

The yew has, for many centuries, been considered as a sacred tree. In ancient Irish mythology, it was one of the five trees brought from the Otherworld when the land was divided. The Druids were said to have revered the yew and therefore planted the trees in close proximity to their temples. Whilst we must remember to approach statements in folklore regarding Druids carefully due to the lack of written records to confirm any of the conjecture, there is probably little to dispute this idea. One of the oldest examples of a churchyard yew, found at Coldwaltham in West Sussex, has been shown to date back to around 1000 BC, which would add credence to the idea that it may have been planted by followers of this religion, although tree experts would point out that the dating of yew is not always an accurate and exact science.

Certainly, it is the case that, as Christianity flourished, the yew was already well-established within places of worship not only across Europe and the Americas, but also at Buddhist temples and Shinto shrines. Pre-Christian religions associated the tree with rebirth or reincarnation. The unusual way that the yew grows is symbolic of this. Yew branches will grow down into the ground where they take hold and produce new stems, which will rise back through the centre of the tree. Over time, the result is several large trunks, all linked in the middle. This new growth from old is an important symbol in terms of the seasonal nature of the world. All the Christian Church did here was "rebrand" the symbolism, moving away from rebirth into the signifying of resurrection. In the UK, the yew is one of the few native evergreens, which would have helped to forge this idea.

This is not the only way that the yew has been seen, though, and there as many associations between the yew and death as there are life and resurrection. This is true, both metaphorically and literally. The Latin genus for the yew, *Taxus,* shares the same root as "toxic," and the tree is certainly that. Each year, a significant number of the area's livestock dies from eating yew leaves, and the bark and seeds are equally as dangerous. It is more difficult for humans to accidentally ingest a fatal amount—you would need fifty grammes of needles for that—but it can happen with intent.

The idea that the yew can bring on hallucinations or altered states of consciousness is not as far-fetched as it might sound. The Greek physician Dioscorides noted that sitting or sleeping in the shade of a yew could be harmful as early as the first century AD. A retired medical professor in the 1970s recalled hallucinating vampires and snakes, amongst other things, after a prolonged period gardening beneath some yew trees.

It is from the seventeenth century onwards that we begin to see the yew being referred to in poetic terms as the "bringer of death." This may be connected to the idea that yew trees in churchyards fed off the corpses that were buried there. This, in turn, possibly emerges from the notion that the roots of the yew would join with the mouths of the bodies buried and transport their souls to the next life, fitting with older cultural ideas of rebirth.

Another key connection between the yew tree and death came about with the realisation that yew staves were perfect for making longbows. The sheer number of lives lost to this weapon in the Middle Ages are staggering. During just one day of the Battle of Agincourt, nearly thirty thousand French soldiers were defeated by only five thousand English archers. Fifty years earlier at Crècy, the seven thousand English archers were capable of firing seventy thousand arrows a minute.

It is a misnomer, however, that yew trees were planted in churchyards in order to help supply the army. It became impossible to sustain the need for yew staves in Britain from native trees alone. Initially, the monarchy imported wood from Spain and across the Irish sea, but even this was not sufficient and, over four centuries, the demand for yew wood almost decimated the European yew population.

So, if they were not planted there to benefit the army, why do we find so many yew trees in churchyards and on consecrated ground (apart from through the links to the older religious practices)?

There are many spiritual reasons for the planting of yew in a churchyard, as we have just seen, but there are practical ones as well. As an evergreen, the tree provides an excellent windbreak, which protects the church building itself from damage. The deliberate planting of these trees would often have their roots (no pun intended) in this idea. In 1307, King Edward I established a statute which required the planting of yew for this purpose, but the idea was most certainly not his own, as a previous ruling put in place by the Synod of Exeter in 1287 forbade the felling of yew trees because of the protection that they offered. Even earlier, in the tenth century, Welsh law levied fines for cutting down *ywen sant* or "saints' yews." A consecrated yew was valued at one pound at this time.

If you were to cut a yew tree, you would find that the wood inside is of two distinct colours, the heartwood being red and the sapwood white. It is easy to see how these colours were once symbolic of the body and blood of Christ, as it is found in the Christian sacrament of Communion.

One ancient yew in the village of Nevern in the Welsh county of Pembrokeshire has a very specific association with blood.

At the sixth-century St Brynach's Church, a yew can be found close to the churchyard gate which exudes a sap the colour and consistency of blood. The tree, whose age has been approximated at seven hundred years, has become known as the "Bleeding Yew of Nevern."

Naturally, folklore has grown around why this particular tree bleeds in this way. One story tells how a monk was wrongfully hanged on the tree, which is now bleeding in protest of his innocence. Another more politically motivated tale says that the tree will bleed until a Welsh Prince has been installed at Nevern, or alternatively until peace has been achieved across the world. There are also more generalised links between the tree and Christian symbolism. The most obvious of these is that the tree bleeds to remind everyone of the crucifixion of Christ. Another symbolic connection is with the Tree of Life, which grew in the Garden of Eden. The last suggestion has a more recent historic link—when the "Mystery Plays" used to be acted out as an educational tool for the transmission of Bible stories, the yew would have played the part of this tree in the story of Adam and Eve.

The yew more broadly was seen to offer supernatural protection, as well as the physical protection of the church building. According to an old German proverb, "beneath yews no magic can persist." Therefore, it was believed that having yew in the boundaries of churchyards would stop spirits from entering the consecrated ground beyond.

Even though the proverb suggests that magic will not survive under a yew, it has not prevented the tree itself from being associated with a number of magical, divinatory, or curative practices.

One of these, of course, is its use in love divination, as there are few plants that have not been used for this purpose at one time or another. Historically, at least, people have always wanted to know who they were going to end up hitched to in order to prepare appropriately. One method was recorded in which a sprig of yew should be picked by a young girl from a churchyard where she has never been before. This sprig should then be taken home and placed under her pillow, leading to her betrothed appearing to her in a dream. However, yew is not the only tree which has been used for this ritual.

Sometimes, yew wood would be burned for a particular purpose. It was believed to be effective in removing negativity and purifying a place, much like sage is used today. The bark, at one time, would also have been burned during Samhain rituals when calling the spirit of an ancestor who has passed.

Across much of central Europe in the Middle Ages, many believed that yew was an ingredient which was effective in an herbal preparation which would help in facilitating abortion. In fact, it was quite a dangerous process, and many women died whilst using this method. Therefore, it might be surprising to find so many yew trees still associated with churches now, as the Church would certainly not have condoned this. However, in the United Kingdom, it was juniper rather than yew which was used as an active ingredient in folk medicine for abortion, and we can find records of juniper trees being felled to try and prevent this use.

With around 1,280 ancient yews in Britain alone, and 72% of these being found in churchyards, it should be no surprise to discover that some of them have their own unique properties in folklore, such as with the Bleeding Yew of Nevern noted above.

The parish church in the Devon village of Stoke Gabriel, the Church of St Mary and St Gabriel, has a yew tree estimated at around a century old, which has a history of magical practice associated with it that was recorded in verse:

"Walk ye backward round about me
Seven times round for all to see
Stumble not and then for certain
One true wish will come to thee"

In some sources, it is suggested that the walker must walk backwards, but this seems to be a later addition, as there is no reference to doing so in the recorded verse. It is likely that this idea had been drawn from the many magical practices and divination rituals which involve circling a church building itself (which are discussed elsewhere in this book). Seven is, of course, a commonly used magical number.

Also in Devon, the Church of All Saints at Culmstock is notable for having a yew growing from the side of its tower. Whilst it doesn't seem to have generated any specific folklore around it, perhaps surprisingly, it has been the cause of much speculation both as to how long it has been there and how it came to be rooted at the top of the building in the first place. It has been variously recorded as two hundred years old, dating back to 1750, and possibly even being from the fourteenth century.

We know from nature studies that birds can take and deposit yew seeds in a variety of inaccessible places, which can cause them to root on steep slopes and the like. Another story connected with these seeds suggests that, when the church spire was removed in 1776 and four weathervanes were installed, yew seeds were mixed with the mortar.

If the tree is old enough to date back to the fourteenth century, then the implication is that it rooted there following a topping out ceremony. The medieval practice took place when a roof was about to be placed on a new building. A yew tree would be tied to the top of the building to dispel any evil spirits before the sealing of the roof. Although less ceremonial, topping out parties are still held in the construction industry today, with a sapling being raised to the new roof with a crane.

At one time, there were other examples known of yew trees growing from church towers. However, these now seem to have died off, and the Culmstock yew appears to be the last of its kind. Though, it is not the only tree to be found growing from the side of a church in this way.

The Cornish church of St Newlyn East has a fig tree growing from its south wall. Legend here relates that the tree grew from a staff which was carried by a Christian princess named Newlina, who had sailed to Cornwall from Ireland. On arriving at Newlyn East after a long walk from where she came ashore at Holywell (a journey which would take her six hours today if she called an Uber), the saint-to-be stuck her staff into the ground and declared that a church should be built on the site. The fig tree grew from the staff.

It seems very likely that this legend is a relatively recent invention, and the prominent motif behind it can be recognised as being not too dissimilar to the story of Joseph of Arimathea and the Glastonbury Thorn. Botanist and folklorist Roy Vickery notes that, in a 1930 study of Cornish trees and shrubs written by Edgar Thurston, the tree is discussed with no reference to the story of Newlina, which seems odd, as Thurston himself was interested in folklore. Also missing from this account is the suggestion that this fig tree is actually cursed.

Anyone picking even the smallest leaf from the tree, it is said, will die within a year as a result of this curse. But, said by whom? A vicar at the church in 1978 told that the tree needed to be cared for from time to time, and "by a remarkable number of coincidences, some of those who have done so have met with misfortune and death." Also, presumably, "some of those who have done so" didn't. Curses don't tend to discriminate.

Another fig tree can be found growing from the wall of another Cornish church, the Church of St Manacca and St Dunstan at Helston. There is a potentially telling link between the two of these in vicar and historian Richard Polwhele, who served at both churches. Polwhele began as vicar of Manaccan in 1794, before moving to St Newlyn East in 1821, where he remained for another seventeen years. It seems highly unusual that a non-native fig should be present at both of his churches.

Occasionally, trees might be found attached to churches without actually growing there. On Royal Oak Day, more commonly known as Oak Apple Day, oak boughs were often attached to the steeples of churches. There are examples of this still surviving in customs in the English county of Wiltshire, as well as at St Neot's church in Cornwall, amongst others. This practice was not for supernatural protection as with the yew, but rather as an act of celebration to remember the escape of King Charles II after the Battle of Worcester in 1651. The king had evaded capture by hiding in an oak tree in the grounds of Boscobel House in Shropshire. After the same fashion, at the London church of St Giles-in-the-Fields, the grave of Richard Penderel, a Roman Catholic farmer and Royalist supporter who had helped the king and chose the tree he used, would be decorated with oak boughs on the anniversary.

In the parts of the United States and Canada where it is native, another evergreen tree takes up the role of the yew. The Eastern Red Cedar is a hardy tree which, whilst not enjoying the substantial longevity of many ancient yews, nonetheless has some well-established examples, such as one in the Methodist Lone Hill Cemetery in Coffee County, Georgia, which is believed to be more than two centuries old.

There are a number of interesting similarities between the yew and the Eastern Red Cedar. In the same way that yew was considered to be sacred, so too is the Red Cedar for many indigenous peoples. The Cherokee, for instance, view the tree in this way because of their belief that the wood holds the spirits of their ancestors. Some tribes use the wood to demarcate hunting territories, with poles fashioned for the purpose.

Its sacred nature means that the cedar is often used for ceremonial purposes. Burning the wood can act as a means of cleansing and purifying and environment, removing negative forces.

The physical properties shared by the Eastern Red Cedar and the yew are remarkably similar. The cedar also has a heartwood which is red in colour, with a much paler sapwood. Interestingly, with correct preparation, the cedar is equally as good as the yew for fashioning bows (including the famed English longbow, which we have already discussed, and indigenous varieties). The cedar also shares symbolic meanings with the yew, with its evergreen needles representing the concept of everlasting life.

Undoubtedly because of its connection with churchyards and grave sites, a lot of the superstition and folklore attached to the Eastern Red Cedar is somewhat negative. Curiously, though, superstitions around the tree in the Ozarks are a little contradictory, as folklore so often is. One old belief here was that, if a Red Cedar that you planted should grow to be tall enough to shade your grave, then you will die. There is some logic to this. The average growth rate of an Eastern Red Cedar is between one and two feet a year, so, if you planted one in early or middle age, then it would indeed be tall enough to shade your grave by the time you were likely to die anyway. Many Ozarkers also believed that it was unlucky to transplant a cedar, as this would bring an early death to the family.

With all this being said, it seems a little surprising that the Red Cedar was, and remains, a popular Christmas tree in many Ozark homes. Maybe its use is designed to regulate the population in the area.

Another evergreen which shares similar characteristics to both the yew and the cedar in terms of its symbolism is the cypress, which is found in churchyards across both Europe and North America, although it was not introduced in the United Kingdom until 1854. The tree's common name, which comes from a combination of French and Latin, finds its origins in the myth of Cyparissos who became very enamoured by a deer, which he subsequently killed by accident whilst on a hunting trip.

To ease his grief and the guilt of what had happened, Apollo, who loved Cyparissos, turned into a tree. This story brings about the associations between grief, loss, and healing in association with the cypress, which is known by some as the "mournful tree."

Foliage from the cypress often finds a use in funeral adornment because of these links, but it has also been used in the winter for cleansing the home of evil spirits, mirroring the yew in this purpose.

Not as common, but still planted in many churchyards, were elder trees. The elder is seen, in terms of folklore, as a protective tree, which is why they would often be planted close to family homes in order to ward off the Devil—which is somewhat ironic, considering that folklore also tells us that burning wood from an elder tree will give one the ability to see the Devil, too. It was said that, if an elder tree in a churchyard was healthy-looking and doing well, it was a sign that the dead buried there were content. This probably links with the fact that a cross, fashioned of elder, would sometimes be placed on the grave of a newly interred corpse, also acting as protection.

In line with other churchyard trees, the elder also has an association with the ideas of rebirth and resurrection. Folklore in some areas says that if an elder tree is felled, another will grow in its place. This idea may well come from the fact that the elder is a simple tree to coppice, with many new stems often growing from a stump.

It's not all positive for the elder in terms of folklore, however. It is known in some circles as the "Judas Tree," because it was said that Judas Iscariot hung himself from an elder—which paints it in a fairly negative light just from the nomenclature. An obscure superstition recorded on the Scottish island of Sanday told that stepping over an elder tree in a churchyard would invite detail within the year. This belief seems to be very localised, as there don't seem to be wider records of it. It presumably refers to the spreading roots of the tree.

Folklore has arisen surrounding some graves which have trees growing from them. When this takes place, the associated stories normally discuss how the person buried there was an atheist, and before death had made some sort of proclamation which said that life after death would only be proven if a tree should sprout from their tomb once they were buried. Many of these trees have long since been removed, undoubtedly because of the underlying damage that they cause to the graves or tombs with which they are associated, but a good example still remains at St Peter's Church in the Hertfordshire village of Tewin.

The grave of Lady Anne Grimston, who died in 1713, was constructed from marble which was fashioned into a tomb. After lying undisturbed for many years, the slab atop this tomb was found to have shifted and cracked. Repairs were fashioned on more than one occasion, but eventually the stonework started to fall apart, and the shoots of a tree could be seen emerging. Further repairs and iron railings could not stop the growth, and, eventually, the tree grew to the enormous size that it is today—a sycamore with four separate trunks.

The normal story applies here in a couple of different variations. In one, Lady Anne is quoted as proclaiming on her deathbed: "I shall not continue to live. It is as unlikely that I shall continue to live as that a tree will grow out of my body. If, indeed, there is life hereafter, trees will rend asunder my tomb." In another version of the story, Lady Anne's words are recorded as "bear witness, my friends, what I say. If there is any truth in the Word of God, may seven trees grow from my grave." It was said at one time that the grave had both a sycamore and an ash growing through it, and that both of these sported seven trunks each, but the only hard evidence that we have now is the four-limbed sycamore.

There is little to suggest that there could be any veracity to this story, which is just one of a number with the same Christian message behind them. It is probably an Edwardian or Victorian invention, as so many of the "morality tales" within folklore are. Historical records suggest that Lady Anne Grimston was perfectly pious and had no reason to doubt the biblical teachings of everlasting life. Furthermore, when you think about it, the legend makes little sense in any case. Considering the length of time that a tree takes to grow and the fact that it was many years before the sapling started to push its way through the tomb, anyone who had heard her last words and would have learned the lesson from the events that unfolded would be long gone (and would have discovered the truth for themselves anyway).

It is far more natural to think about flowers on graves than it is trees, but, in fact, the act of placing flowers on family plots in churchyards and cemeteries—be it for remembrance or anything else—is more recent than many might guess. It did not become particularly common until the early nineteenth century, around the same time that large and well-tended municipal cemeteries began to be constructed.

Prior to approximately 1830, the custom of placing flowers on graves was predominantly found in Wales. These were not placed in receptacles like we might today, but were strewn over the grave, along with evergreen foliage—the same also being used to decorate the church. This act would take place immediately following a funeral, and then a number of times in the year following. It was important that the flowers used for this were pleasantly scented.

Of course, the same village arguments and prejudices could very easily be played out after death, as well as before it. There were cases in which the graves of people who had not been well-liked in life were strewn just as liberally with thistles or nettles as the other graves were with pinks and carnations.

Another similar custom in Wales used to take place on the day before Palm Sunday, when graves were tied and flowers refreshed. It is probable that this practice was originally tied to a geographically distinct area of the southeast of Wales, with a little leaching over the border into England, but then gradually spread out across more of Wales. In Welsh, this custom is known as *Sul y Blodau,* which translates to "Flowering Sunday." It was sometimes associated with other times of the year, such as Easter Sunday, but the name has now become synonymous in Wales with Palm Sunday.

Marking the start of Holy Week and celebrating Christ's entry into Jerusalem for those of that faith, Palm Sunday is an important moveable feast on the Christian calendar. The Bible describes how watchers covered the road both with their cloaks and locally cut brushwood, which has generally been considered to be palm, hence the name.

Many churches make and distribute small palm crosses on this day, which, in recent times, are usually made of date palm. Before this was easily imported, other plants would have substituted for the biblical "palm," including pussy willow in England and the churchyard trees of cypress and yew in Ireland. Branches of the latter were often given out in Catholic mass to the congregation and could be taken and used at home in order to invite good luck to the house. In some Palm Sunday services, palm branches, or fronds, would be carried in procession before being placed on the altar to be blessed prior to their distribution.

Before churches commonly had stone floors—flagging being quite widespread by the start of the nineteenth century—earthen floors would be covered and renewed frequently. This practice led to an ecclesiastical custom known as "rushbearing," which is no longer extant through continuity, but still exists in some parts of the north of England through revivalism.

In the Middle Ages, most churches chose one day a year for their rushbearing, and over time, this developed into a celebration, with the church bells being rung and refreshments provided for those doing the work. In more elaborate festivals, there might be music and traditional morris dancing, and sometimes a form of play or pageant. This meant that they inevitably became a good excuse for heavy drinking, petty theft, and everything else that you might expect from a medieval party.

Rushes were often strewn in the church on feast days, and sometimes particular fragrant plants were used in order to improve the smell of the church, as well as for their insulating properties. Norwich Cathedral usually used sweet flag on rush-bearing feast days; it is amusing to note that it is also known for its psychoactive chemicals, although records do not indicate an increase in religious visions at this church.

Other locations used more humble plants. The parish of Middleton-Cheney in Northamptonshire used hay, which was provided in the summer through a benefaction, but was replaced with straw provided by the vicar of the church himself in the winter. At the other end of the social scale, at Hampton Court in the sixteenth century, Cardinal Wolsey would have the rushes renewed every day.

Thomas Noble, in his *History of the County of Derbyshire* gave an account of rushbearings in the area as they would have taken place just before the custom died out:

> *It usually takes place at the latter end of August, on public notice from the churchwardens, of the rushes being mown and properly dried, in some marshy part of the parish, where the young people assemble: the carts are loaded with rushes and with flowers and ribands; and are attended to the church by the populous, many huzzaing and cracking whips by the side of the rush-cart, on their way thither, where everyone lends a hand in carrying in and spreading the rushes.*

Probably the most well-known of the revivals for rushbearing is the Saddleworth Rushcart, which takes place on the late August Bank Holiday weekend at Saddleworth in West Yorkshire. The custom here was reconstructed by the local morris dance side and involves the gathering of rushes, which are then piled onto a colourfully decorated two-wheeled cart. The pile of rushes reaches some twelve or thirteen feet in height, on top of which sits a member of the dancers known as a "jockey." The cart is paraded around local villages on the Saturday, and then, on the Sunday, is taken to St Chad's Church at Uppermill, where the rushes are then strewn. Morris dancers from all over Britain travel to join the Saddleworth side and be part of the event.

In his 1891 book named after the above practice, *Rushbearing*, Alfred Burton also described another custom which still carries on to this day, taking place every year on May 29 (unless that date falls on a Sunday, in which it is moved to the day before or after). That event is Castleton Garland Day, which may be found in Castleton, in Derbyshire.

The Garland Day ceremony is possibly connected with Royal Oak Day, or Oak Apple Day, which we discussed earlier in this chapter. In this case, the garland would be representative of the oak tree which concealed the king. However, there is an alternative origin which could be much older. For a large part of the procession, which is led by a "Garland King" and his concert, the king is decked with a large framework covered in flowers—the "garland for which the ceremony is named"—and this whole construct is very reminiscent of a Jack in the Green.

The ceremony remains largely unchanged to this day from when it was first observed and recorded in 1885 by Alfred Burton. He wrote:

> *The framework is of wood, thatched with straw. Interior diameter, a little over two feet, outside (when covered with flowers) over three feet six inches. In shape, it somewhat resembles a bell, completely covered over with wild flowers[sic] (…) The top, called the 'queen' is formed of garden flowers, and fits into a socket at the top of the garland. It weighs over a hundredweight, requires two men to lift it, and has occupied four men from noon till five o'clock in the afternoon to make it.*
>
> *(The garland) is bourne on the head and shoulders of a man riding a horse, and wearing a red jacket. A stout handle inside, which rests on the saddle in front of him, enables him to hold it upright. It completely envelopes him to the waist… After parading the village, the 'queen' is taken off the garland and placed in the church, the garland being hoisted with ropes to the top of the church tower, where it is placed on one of the pinnacles, and left till it has withered away, when the framework is taken down and kept for another year. The other pinnacles have branches of oak.*

It is this latter note which highlights the similarity of this custom to elements of Oak Apple Day. So, is this the origin, or is the ceremony drawn from May Day festivities more closely linked to the Jack in the Green? The answer to that question is down to the individual reader to decide.

When we examine the records kept by wardens of the church, it is clear that many plants used to be grown in the churchyard, and these were subsequently used for church decoration. A number of these plants were connected with certain times of the year and important feast days. Holly and ivy would naturally be cut and brought into the church at Christmas. Roses would be used both for St Martin's Day and for Corpus Christi. Red and white flowers would be used on certain occasions. This might be seen as being symbolic of the sacrament, the body and blood of Christ, but also representing love and wisdom.

The Reformation altered the design of many churches drastically, with the removal of icons and statues, the whitewashing of walls, and an emphasis on simplicity. Because of this, many maintained gardens in churchyards then also began to become unkempt and their plants overlooked.

Particular plants may be banned from churches at certain times of the year. In the Advent period, the four Sundays before Christmas, a focus is placed on the build-up to the birth of Christ on Christmas Day. Floral decorations are often removed from churches at this time, instead being replaced with an Advent wreath which is made up of greenery from the churchyard. Candles are often incorporated into this wreath, with one being lit on each Sunday, with the final central candle being set to flame on December 25 itself, or at the Midnight Mass leading into that day. Often, using the same symbolism, the advent candles will be red and the final one white.

Also connected with Christmas traditions is mistletoe, a parasitic plant which can often be found clumping in other trees. There have been occasions in the past where this plant had been banned from churches in the festive period, usually by overzealous vicars who have little understanding of the stories that surround it.

An example of this was printed in the *Daily Mirror* newspaper in 1958, which reported:

> *The ban announced by the Reverend H.R. Joyce applies to St[sic] Thomas's Church, Derby. He has invited parishioners to decorate the church with holly,[sic] but has told them 'Mistletoe is a pagan decoration and under no circumstances should be hung in a Christian church'. He explained yesterday: 'Mistletoe has strong connections with the Druids, who were pagan leaders of the Ancient Britons'.*

The idea of the Druids treating mistletoe has been oft repeated, but, as we have noted elsewhere, it is impossible to verify many of the ideas associated with what the Druids did or did not find sacred because of a lack of written records to testify to the facts. As early as the first century AD, Pliny the Elder had made the suggestion that mistletoe was sacred to the Druids, and especially so when it was found growing on oak trees. However, the plant is rarely found as a parasite to the oak. A two-year study carried out in Britain in recent years found just over a dozen such trees exist across the whole country.

One flower which is certainly synonymous with churchyards, as the chill of winter moves towards the warmth of spring, is the snowdrop. Many a country church sport blankets of snowdrops in its grounds, enjoying the shade found beneath the yew trees and breaking through the frosty covering of the soil. A nineteenth-century English floral calendar suggested that the snowdrop first rears its head on Candlemas Day—and indeed, village girls in Yorkshire would once gather bunches of snowdrops and wear them on this day as a symbol of purity, although this does suggest that the flowers reared their heads well in advance of Candlemas to be ready for picking at this time.

The placing of candles at the feet of statues of the Virgin Mary at this time led to one of the colloquial names for the snowdrop—Mary's Tapers—although it has many other ones, such as Candlemas Bells (named for the shape of the flower head) and Corpse Flower. The latter name makes reference to the idea that soldiers from the Crimean War saw the flowers on the battlefields there and brought them back to Britain to plant.

It was the Victorians who began planting large numbers of snowdrops in churchyards, perhaps picking up on this association themselves, and it is at this time that we see a number of superstitions detailing the reasons why it was said to be bad luck to bring snowdrops into the house. Amongst these concerns were that the flowers would affect that quality of a cow's milk (and, therefore, butter), as well as the number of eggs that a sitting hen would successfully hatch. In a worst-case scenario, bringing snowdrops into the home could invite death to follow.

Snowdrops, of course, were not alone in this, and there are a number of plants and flowers which have similar negative connotations surrounding the time of year that they are brought into the house and what harm they may cause.

Through Christian associations, the snowdrop is also linked to the creation myth and Adam and Eve's ejection from the Garden of Eden. An angel that appears to the couple first turns snowflakes into the small white flowers before offering to take them out into the world as a sign of hope. Earlier than this, there are similar Pagan associations with purity, health, and hope—the green of the stem being symbolic of the wellbeing aspect and the white flowerhead reminding us of the strengthening of the sun as spring approaches and life begins to return to the soil.

Soil itself might sometimes be thought of as containing magical properties and can appear in folk remedies, as well as the actual plants which might be harvested for this purpose. Consider, for example, the soil in a particular part of the churchyard at Sacred Heart Roman Catholic Church in the hamlet of Boho at County Fermanagh in Ireland.

The soil in question makes up the grave of the Reverend James McGirr who was the parish priest here at the beginning of the nineteenth century. It was said that Reverend McGirr once declared "after I die, the clay that covers me will cure anything that I cured when I was with you." The vicar was obviously known for his ability to cure illness in life, so the tradition began of visiting the grave and taking a small amount of soil. This should then be wrapped in a piece of cloth and placed under the pillow of the sufferer.

There is a very practical part to this superstitious folk remedy, in that, after saying prayers, it was important for the soil to be returned to the grave in order for the cure to be effective. This explains how people are still able to practice this ritual today, the grave soil being self-replenishing because of this part of the superstition.

Although many folk remedies are steeped in superstition, there are often very sound pieces of medical reasoning behind them. This is also the case with the soil from Reverend McGirr's grave, which was tested by microbiologist Dr. Gerry Quinn who was interested to know whether there was any truth behind the belief.

Analysing the soil from the grave led Dr. Quinn to discover that it contained a unique strain of *Streptomyces* which was not known anywhere else. *Streptomyces* is the organism which lies at the heart of antibiotics, and new strains are vital in the fight against bacteria that, over time, become resistant to existing antibiotics. This particular strain was found to be effective at eliminating the top three disease-bearing organisms which the World Health Organisation had listed as being a threat to humans.

Dr. Quinn had first pursued the idea of examining this soil because of the underlying folk tradition, realising that, for something to persist for two hundred years, there had to be some element of truth or efficacy behind it. This view provides a good reason for looking more closely at many other folk remedies and traditional knowledge of healing and medicine. However, getting conclusive results in this way is somewhat time-limited.

As the world becomes increasingly globalised and modern, not only are some of the flora and fauna that lend themselves to folk medicines at risk, but so too is the knowledge about how they should be used. Indigenous ethnic groups, along with the kinds of oral transmission and community structures which preserve this material, are increasingly under threat of destruction in different ways—and with their loss also comes the loss of such knowledge. Make a note—this is just one of many reasons why folklore is so important.

An unusual story tells of an unnamed herb which grew in the churchyard at Bonamargy Friary, on the Irish coast at County Antrim. Originally a Franciscan friary, Bonamargy was dissolved in 1584 and, five years later, suffered fire damage whilst being occupied by the British army. Today, the site, which is reputed to be haunted by a ghost known as the "Black Nun," is open to the public. The church and graveyard are still there, although the cloister is now only ruins.

In the rather obscure tale, knowledge about the healing properties of this particular herb came to be told to a man who lived on the nearby island of Rathlin, which lies about six miles from the mainland. The man had gone out from his house to a nearby well to fetch water in order to boil potatoes for a meal. His wife suffered from rheumatism and had been unable to make the journey herself. Having fetched the water, returned home, and set the potatoes to boiling over the fire, the man went back out of the house to walk. It was at this point that he came across an unusual procession.

In front of him were a passing party of fairies bearing a casket, which he took to be a coffin. He did not approach the party himself, but one of the fairies spoke to him, having been able to discern what was on the man's mind—namely, his wife's condition. The fairy told the man that an herb grew in the churchyard over the water at Bonamargy which was very effective at relieving pain. Not knowing where to find it, the man asked if the fairies could show him where he should go to collect the herb—so they magically transported him across the water. After gathering some of the plant, the fairies returned the man to the island once again. All of this happened in such a short space of time that the man's wife had not even noticed his absence.

The story is very vague and definitely fits into the folk tale category, so we have no idea what the herb in question was, or whether Bonamargy was the only churchyard in which it could be found. Perhaps this particular plant was betony, which was thought of by herbalists in the Middle Ages as a general cure-all.

Betony, whose Latin name is *Betonica officinalis,* is a plant which is found more often these days in churchyards than it is in the countryside, at least in Britain (although it is native to most of Europe, as well as parts of both Africa and Asia). The epithet *officinalis* makes reference to the types of plants which are known to have uses in medicine. Betony was known to be an ingredient in Pistoia powder, which was used in the treatment of arthritis and gout, which might form a link to the fairy story from Bonamargy.

We cannot underestimate the sheer number of uses of betony which lead to it being considered as a cure-all. Seventeenth-century herbalist Nicholas Culpeper listed these as:

> *Epidemical Diseases, Witchcraft, Apetite, Indigestion, Stomach, Belching, Jaundice, Falling-sickness, Palsey, Convulsion, Shrinking of the Sinews, Gout, Dropsie, Frensie, Cough, Cold, Shortness of Breath, Agues of all sorts, Sore Eyes, Worms, Obstructions of the Liver and Spleen, Stitches, Pains in the Back and Belly, Terms provokes, Mother, Childbirth Stone, Toothache, Venemous Beasts, Mad-dogs, Weariness, Bleeding at Mouth and Nose, Pissing & spitting of Blood, Ruptures, Bruises, Wounds, Veins and Sinews Cut, Ulcers, Fistulaes, Boyls, Ears.*

Culpeper includes Witchcraft here as a disease which can be treated, and he was not alone in using betony for this purpose.

Antonius Musa, Emperor Augustus's physician and a botanist in his own right, also believed that betony was effective against forms of sorcery, and it is possibly because of this that we find it in a number of churchyards now. It was thought that the plant was good at protecting against ghosts and other supernatural threats.

Whilst there is a wide range of flora and fauna to be found in our churchyards which can be seen to have folklore attached to them in differing ways, there is one surprising common plant to be found there which has almost none. Considering its proliferation, this is perhaps equally surprising in itself. That plant is lichen.

Since they have no root systems, and therefore no need to take nutrients from the soil, lichens may be found attached to many different surfaces and, in particular, they will commonly be seen on old gravestones and the sides of churches themselves. One reason, perhaps, for their prevalence in these spaces is the fact that churches tend to often be set apart from the rest of a community and do not enjoy the same sorts of passing traffic. Lichen has no ability to differentiate between good and bad chemicals, so it will thrive more in places with good air quality.

There are three different biological groups of lichens, of which crustose lichen is the one most commonly found attached to gravestones and similar flat surfaces. The plant grips very tightly to the surface, a little like a limpet, attaches itself to a rock and is very difficult to remove without causing damage to the surface of the stone. For this reason, many of the old gravestones dating back to the eighteenth century or earlier may be covered with lichen which is almost as old as the fashioned stone itself.

Medieval doctors would use lichen as a treatment for skin conditions. At the time, it was common to use plants which bore some resemblance to either the part of the body or the ailment which was being treated. As such, lichens, which look like crusted or peeling skin, would be used in the treatment of such conditions. As we found with the soil of Reverend McGirr's grave, occasionally there is some science to be found amongst the superstition. Many lichens are known to have antibacterial properties to them, although they are not often used in conventional medical treatments today.

Let's close this chapter in the way that we started it: with some lines of poetry. This time, from the American romantic poet William Cullen Bryant, who was known for his nature writings and his description of a traditional English churchyard:

Erewhile on England's pleasant shores, our sires
Left not their churchyards unadorned with shades
Or blossoms; and, indulgent to the strong
And natural dread of man's last home – the grave!
Its frost and silence, they disposed around,
Too sadly on life's close, the forms and hues
Of vegetable beauty. Then the Yew,
Green even amid the snows of Winter, told
Of immortality; and gracefully
The Willow, a perpetual mourner, drooped;
And there the gadding Woodbine crept about;
And there the ancient Ivy.

CHAPTER FOUR

PAGAN SYMBOLS IN THE CHURCH

THE MEDIEVAL CHURCH OF ALL SAINTS can be found at Braunston in Rutland. With its earliest parts dating from the twelfth century, the building is adorned with some valuable wall paintings from the fourteen hundreds and is home to many important historical features, including a stone grave covering which has a Nine Men's Morris board incised into it. Nine Men's Morris is a strategic game for two people which can be traced back to Roman times.

After so many centuries of transit (allowing people entry to and egress from the church), the doorstep of All Saints' Church naturally began to wear. So, in 1920, it was decided that it should be replaced. Church authorities, however, were in for an unexpected surprise when the stone was lifted. The underside of what had been the church doorstep was carved with a curious female form.

The Braunston figure had two eyes with recessed pupils (although only one now remains), a strange double nose, and large mouth, in which a tongue is clearly visible. Running horizontally from the mouth down to the chest are deep striations, ending at a pair of breasts. The stone is carved on three sides, with the flat side to the rear having been the side that faced up as a doorstep. A strange figure indeed, and one having no obvious connections to a Christian church. However, as we shall learn in this chapter, secular imagery and folk art in churches and churchyards is plentiful.

The figure has become commonly known by a couple of different names, both of which are unhelpful in terms of ascertaining the folklore or symbolism of the stone. It is often referred to as the "Braunston Goddess," but (outside of the pair of well-rounded breasts) there is nothing to evidence this name. Saxon and Norman experts, as well as medievalists, have all failed to pin the figure to any of their timelines.

In other places, including the website for the church itself, the figure has been called a "Shelagh," after the symbolism of the *sheela na gigs* found carved into many historic churches and other non-religious buildings in the United Kingdom, as well as other countries. The sheela na gig resembles a bald female, usually naked, sitting with splayed legs and holding a parted vulva.

The origins of the sheela are far from clear. Most carvings seem to originate from a period of around four hundred years between the twelfth and sixteenth centuries, but this doesn't mean that there are not older examples. The name is equally mysterious with respect to its etymology. In Ireland, the term would be applied to some women who were said to expose themselves to ward off the evil eye. In this sense, the sheela could almost be seen as an apotropaic figure.

There is a much broader collection of legends from across the world of women exposing their genitals to drive away evil. Tamer versions of these stories can be found in relation to wars and armadas, where local women were said to have gathered on cliff tops and lifted their skirts to show petticoats of a particular colour, matching the livery of soldiers from that country. Their actions, when viewed from afar, would allegedly cause ships to turn around in the mistaken belief that there were far more army personnel ready to engage them than were actually there.

Some church sheelas are found in doorways, which seems to suggest a more protective aspect, perhaps mirroring this aspect of driving away evil.

The problem, of course, with the Braunston carving is that it has no genitalia, and so cannot truly be described as a sheela na gig in that sense. One interesting suggestion offered about the figure is that it was once a Hunky Punk.

Hunky Punks are a variation of the grotesque church adornments discussed in Chapter One. They are generally associated with churches found in the English county of Somerset, and they jut out at an angle from the church towers, often at an upward angle from the corners.

This idea is an intriguing one. Potentially in its favour is the fact that striations are a common adornment to church grotesques. Also, if the Braunston carving is turned upside down to stand on its head, it then resembles a male figure, with the breasts becoming the eyes. This is the direction in which it would be viewed from if it were originally a Hunky Punk.

The Braunston "Shelagh" is not alone in having been found buried upside down in a church in this way. A genuine sheela na gig was discovered in this way at the Old Parish Church in Llandrindod, Wales. This is an especially rare carving, as there is only one other definitely identified sheela in Wales (with a couple of other carvings for which there is a little more speculation as evidence).

There is really no one-size-fits-all explanation for the curious image of the sheela na gig, although it is quite easy to accept that one wouldn't expect to see such a representation in a church. For this reason, one suggested explanation is that of a warning against the sins of lust. However, this can be somewhat easily discounted across the board, as there are many examples of figures on buildings with no religious significance. On the other hand, a similar, although inverted, argument works against the idea of the sheela being a fertility symbol.

The sheela is often adopted as a purely Pagan symbol, leading to suggestions that she is a surviving element of goddess worship, but this seems far from clear-cut. There is no firm evidence to show the age of the sheela in terms of an origin point, and, therefore, no traceable lineage in this way.

It is most likely that the figure has been associated with aspects of all of these, but not where it comes from. The more logical theory points to it being a protector, keeping the church or other buildings safe from supernatural incursion and danger, in much the same way as a church grim.

Apotropaic markings were frequently used in both large country houses and more modest homes as another prevention against supernatural threats. Carvings were often incised into stonework or wood as a way of fighting magic with magic—we find many examples of this in churches as well, often being called "medieval graffiti." When surveying such things, however, we do need to be mindful of the distinctions between apotropaic protection marks and more normal mason's or carpenter's marks. The mason's mark worked a little like a hallmark and were used to identify which stonemason had worked on a piece of stone, whereas the latter often took the form of Roman numerals which indicated the ways in which pieces of wood should be fitted together to make frames or other structures—sort of like medieval Ikea assembly instructions, without the leftover screw at the end.

Of the various types of apotropaic marks that were used, the one with the closest links to the church is probably the "Marian" mark. Consisting of two overlapping V shapes, these are believed to form the letter M as an invocation of the Virgin Mary for protection. In pre-Reformation times, Mary was oft venerated, so these marks would have been quite commonly used at this time.

Perhaps the most common of all protective marks is the daisy wheel, or "hexafoil." It is a geometric shape that can be easily drawn with a compass, inscribing an outer circular border inside of which a six-pointed rosette is formed with sections of circle of the same circumference. They may be found with equal frequency on both stone and woodwork, and there are numerous examples in churches across the world.

These marks would often be placed in boundary points to protect the whole building, such as door lintels, fireplace lintels, or in roof spaces. Others may offer more personal protection. In the Derbyshire town of Ashbourne, All Saints' Church features a good example in the wood on the end of a church pew in its side chapel. Perhaps this was placed there to protect members of a particular family, as, historically, some families would have their own pews in churches.

Hexafoils also have a long history in a mortuary context and can be found on a number of old gravestones, particularly on Roman gravestones across Europe. Equally early examples appear on the sides of Jewish ossuary boxes from a century before the birth of Christ, indicating that we should not consider this symbol to be from a Christian context. Ossuaries were stone boxes into which human remains were placed before being interred. It is certainly associated with non-Christian gods in Slavic folklore, for instance. The hexafoils would have served to protect the deceased on the road to the afterlife or later, as they awaited resurrection.

It is believed by some that the power with which a hexafoil is imbued resembles the same power which is found in Solomon's Knot, a symbol which was etched into King Solomon's ring. This "knot" is made up of a line which appears to be endless, is said to have been engraved by God, and serves to trap evil within it. The hexafoil may also be derived from much older solar symbols which combatted darkness through light, although the evidence for this is perhaps more speculative.

The meaning behind graffiti marks such as these in churches are not always easy to discern and can be ambiguous. At the church of St Mary the Virgin in the village of Chalk, in Kent, graffiti in the form of the outline of two shoes was found incised into a decorated lead wall plaque containing bas-relief figures. As there was a well-established protective ritual surrounding the placement of concealed shoes in old buildings, it might be tempting to consider that these outlines—one square-toed shoe and one with a pointed end—might serve the same purpose.

Local folklore suggests that the footprints belonged to an important local landowner from the eighteenth century named William Brown. However, if this were the case, then we would expect the two shoes to match—if he was a major landowner, he could surely afford a decent pair of matching shoes.

It is probable, though, that this is a commemoration graffiti example. Church patrons would often be recognised in the building works which they funded, and a shoe print could act as a signature. Often, the shoe of a member of the church would also be outlined to "ratify" the first. In this case, maybe one of the shoes belonged to a patron—and perhaps that was William Brown—and the other to a vicar or curate. Both shoe prints have dedications on them, but they are very indistinct, although one appears to be dated to 1758.

Burn marks were often deliberately made into timbers, and these most definitely are apotropaic, acting as a form of protection against the supernatural. They are often called *taper burns*, but this is not a great description, as many of the marks of a larger size would not have been made with tapers. Candles or other naked flames were equally as effective and would have been more easily accessible in many cases.

Sometimes, these apotropaic marks can cross over into other aspects of folklore, and this is the case with what is arguably the best-known example of deliberate burn marks in a church environment. These are found on the inside of one of the doors of the fifteenth-century Holy Trinity Church at Blythborough in Suffolk, which, at least according to legend, was attacked by a terrifying black dog during a thunderstorm in August of

1577. The story is linked to another at nearby Bungay, which still celebrates its connection to the black dog to this day.

Historical documents tell us that lightning "cleft the door, and returning to the steeple, rent the timber, brake*[sic]* the chimes, and fled towards Bongay, six miles off." A forty-year-old man and a boy aged fifteen were killed as a result of the strike. The folklore surrounding the black dog leaving its scorched claw marks in the church door soon arose, thanks in part to a now well-known pamphlet written by English clergyman Abraham Fleming after the event. However, some people also refer to the burn marks as the fingerprints of the Devil. Both versions are somewhat ironic, considering the true nature of the marks is to offer protection to the building.

The story of the black dog (or the Devil) visiting the church rises from a thunderstorm and lightning phenomenon which is very similar to one some sixty years later which occurred at the Church of St Pancras in the Dartmoor town of Widecombe in the Moor. Coincidentally, Holy Trinity Church at Blythborough is also known as the "Cathedral of the Marshes" because of its unusual size for an area with such a small population, and the church of St Pancras as "The Cathedral of the Moor" for its similarly impressive architecture. We will discover more about the Widecombe storm and its folklore in Chapter Six when we meet the Devil.

A very unexpected symbol to be found in some Christian churches is that of the pentagram, due to its current strong connections and connotations within Witchcraft of various types. However, in the early modern period, the pentagram was used by Christians as being symbolic of the five wounds of Christ, and the term five-pointed star would have been used for the symbol.

The examples of pentagrams that we find in churches will sometimes be inverted; this mirrors the practice used in art of the symbol being positioned above or atop a demon, pinning it down and, therefore, destroying its power. There is a fine example of such a "demon trap" in the fourteenth-century Church of St Mary at Troston in Bury St Edmunds.

The Troston Demon, as it is often known, probably dates from around 1350 and takes the form of a somewhat cartoonish, grotesque screaming figure with wide eyes and an oversized tongue. Over the top of this, a pentacle has been incised, which shows signs that suggest it has been repeatedly recut over the years. In fact, it has now become something of a tradition locally to renew the protection that the pentagram gives by cutting it again. It can be found on the east side of the chancel. A number of hexafoils have also been found in this church.

Again, we have to exercise some caution with interpretation of the pentagram, or five-pointed star, in a Church context, as the symbol was often also used as a mason's mark. In the Arthurian legend of Gawain and the Green Knight, a five-pointed star was prominent on Gawain's shield.

Another numerically significant symbol which became associated with churches is the rotationally symmetrical triplicate motif known as the "triskelion." This is often made up of three interlocking spirals coming from a common central point, although other shapes can sometimes replace the spirals in different contexts. We might think of the symbol on some flags, such as the three legs on that from the Isle of Man, for example.

The triskelion's history is particularly old, and examples can be traced back thousands of years. It is frequently associated with Celtic symbolism, but this is a misattribution. Examples found at the Stone Age passage tomb of Newgrange in Ireland are over five thousand years old, an age which means that they pre-date the Celts arriving in the country by some two and a half centuries.

It is certainly true that the triple spiral triskelion symbol is often found on artefacts belonging to the Celts, both ceremonial and objects which would have been used in everyday life. This fact suggests that these people adopted the earlier image for their own purposes.

The Roman Empire's overcoming of the Celts did not erase the triskelion from history in the way that it removed many of their other traditional practices, and, by the thirteenth century, the motif started to appear in church architecture. It would become more common as a part of the stonework in church window designs, particularly in Gothic architecture across Europe.

There is a particularly good example to be found in the town of Avioth in the northeast of France, as part of a small chapel called *La Recevresse* which stands outside the cemetery wall of the grand church of Our Lady's Basilica. The chapel is built in a particularly ornate Gothic style. Its name translates as "The Receiver" and came about because pilgrims who were making their way to the main church began leaving offerings at the chapel. This then developed into an ongoing custom.

As it became more closely associated with the Christian faith, the triskelion started to be interpreted in terms of a representation of the Holy Trinity, comprised of God, Jesus Christ, and the Holy Spirit. However, as the symbol is much older than this, there have naturally been a number of other permutations of its representation.

On a basic level, the motif can be thought of as representing the cycles of human life: beginning with birth, moving on to the journey through life, and culminating with death at the end of the path. A more spiritual reading of the symbols suggests three possible planes of existence. One arm, or spiral, would represent the spirit world of the heavens, another the mortal dwelling place of Earth, and the third, the demonic underworld of eternal damnation below.

A final, more nature-based interpretation might view the triskelion as representing three of the elements: Earth, Water, and Sky (or Air). This more Pagan reading leads us to another variant of the triskele, which is very common in secular church architecture, but which also has a much broader pre-Christian longevity behind it. That is the symbol of the three hares.

Made using the same threefold rotational symmetry as the more geometric versions, this version of the triskelion consists of three hares, joined at the ear-tips and running in an endless circle. It is a clever piece of design; only three ears are present, but the image is constructed in such a way that each hare still appears to have two ears.

This motif has a very long past. The earliest example that we know of dates from AD 600 and was found in a cave in China. Other particularly early examples come from Afghanistan in 1100 and Nepal in 1200. It probably found its way into Europe along the Spice Road and other trade routes, as many other folkloric icons and stories have.

The image appears in a number of churches but is not as widespread as other triskelions. A particularly fine example from the Middle Ages is depicted in stained glass on a roundel above the north door of Holy Trinity Church at Long Melford in the English county of Suffolk. Building of this church was completed in 1484 and the window has survived well, with some damage from the Cromwellian era having been repaired sympathetically.

Much like the more abstract triskelion, interpretation of the three hares motif within the context of church buildings generally centres around a reading as a depiction of the Holy Trinity. In older belief systems, there are different connections. Regarding the earliest example from China, in this country's mythology, the hare is symbolic of the resurrection and is connected with the moon. The hare in the moon (their version of our "man in the moon") was said to crush herbs of immortality. Similar interpretations can be found in India and Egypt. Across Europe, there seems to have been a cult of the hare goddess, but, evidentially, linking this to the motif of the three hares with any certainty is tenuous.

Excavations of the nave at Chester cathedral in 1996 unearthed a floor tile dated to the fourteenth century, which, again, depicted the three hares motif. The tile is now held at the Grosvenor Museum. The three hares symbol is quite rare generally across Britain as a piece of church iconography, but there is an unusually large concentration in the county of Devon, with some twenty-eight known examples.

Many of the Devon three hares can be found in churches on Dartmoor, a national park which is known, amongst other things, for its extensive tin mining history. Tinners on Dartmoor existed almost within their own society, governed by their own laws administered through stannary parliaments.

The three hares symbol on Dartmoor is usually referred to as the "Tinner's Rabbits." This is a misnomer. The animals are neither rabbits, nor do they have any connection with the tinners. Yet, the symbol is often used in this way in modern installations, which causes the association to perpetuate. The Castle Inn at Lydford, for example, used the symbol in a new piece of stained glass in the part of the establishment called "The Tinner's Bar."

Most likely responsible for making the link between the three hares and the tinners, which is actually quite recent, is Lady Sylvia Sayer. Lady Sayer was a past chair and patron of the Dartmoor National Park Authority who campaigned tirelessly on issues surrounding conservation and the environment in the area. In 1951, her book *The Outline of Dartmoor's Story* was published, which stated:

> *The Fifteenth century was a particularly prosperous time for Dartmoor tinners, and by way of a thank-offering they enlarged and rebuilt some of the moorland churches. Widecombe church is a fine example, and there you can see the tinners' emblem carved on a roof-boss* –[sic] *three rabbits sharing ears...*

The word "emblem" here suggests that the three hares was used as a badge by the tinners, for which there is no evidence at all.

Sylvia Sayer is not the only "Lady" who has provided some misattribution of ideas to folkloric imagery through her writing. Another, Julia Somerset—Lady Raglan—contributed greatly to the conflation of ideas surrounding one of the most iconic secular images within churches, the foliate heads that we now generally describe using the phrase "green man."

The image of the head disgorging vegetation appears in large numbers of church buildings, and there have been many surveys undertaken of these. Discussion of the symbol and its interpretation can, and does, form books in their own right, and, as such, this is not the place to repeat such extensive work. However, it is important to unpick some of the folklore and interpretation to try and separate the facts from the speculation.

Like the three hares, the image of the foliate head has very early starting points, with second-century examples found in Iraq and Lebanon, and other early-century examples from India and across Asia. They likely entered English architecture around the twelfth century, although there are much earlier examples in Europe, such as the carving on the tomb of St Abre at the Church of St Hilaire in Poitiers, France, which is dated somewhere between the fourth and sixth centuries.

The foliate head symbol is generally associated with ideas of rebirth. It is occasionally connected with vegetation deities, but its origins are naturally blurred. It most probably emerges from Roman art, where leaf masks were used to represent mythological gods. As with some of the other symbolism that we have explored in this book, in a church context, the rebirth association becomes resurrection. In medieval legend, Seth places three seeds in Adam's mouth, from which sprout what becomes the tree of life, and links have been made between some foliate heads and this story.

We can thank Lady Raglan for the term "green man." It comes from a paper which she wrote called "The Green Man in Church Architecture," which was published in the journal of the Folklore Society, *Folklore,* in March 1939. In it, she explains how she learned of the figure and coined the name:

> *It is now about eight years since my attention was first drawn by the Revd. J. Griffith, then vicar of Llangwm, in Monmouthshire, and himself a folklorist, to a curious carving. It is*

> *a man's face, with oak leaves growing from the mouth and ears, and completely encircling the head. Mr*[**sic**] *Griffith suggested that it was intended to symbolise the spirit of inspiration, but it seemed to me certain that it was a man and not a spirit, and moreover that it was a Green Man. So I named it, and the evidence that I have collected to support this title is the reason for this paper.*

Unfortunately, our issues here must first lie with the word "evidence." In much the same vein as Margaret Murray's broadly discredited work on the pervading history of a witch cult from Pagan times was based on supposition and conjecture, not on actual proof, so is Lady Raglan's work when she suggests that the green man, to which she refers in the church, is connected with the Jack in the Green, as well as figures such as Robin Hood.

Many articles suggest that all of the iterations of the green man are linked in some way and, while it may be the case, it is unlikely that the link is really any stronger than the fact that, in their own ways, they all reference the idea of the nature spirit (which is such a powerful motif generally).

The earliest naming of the green man really refers to the characters often known as "whifflers" who would walk at the heads of processions in Tudor and Elizabethan times to clear crowds out of the way—kind of a Middle Age's equivalent of the man with a red flag walking in front of early motor vehicles to warn pedestrians of the approaching danger. The whiffler's dress was often as a savage man or a wild man (a figure who we shall shortly see making a surprising appearance in a church himself), but sometimes they would be covered in foliage and would be referred to as green men instead.

Jack in the Green processions, which have also been linked to the image of the foliate head thanks to Lady Raglan, refer to an annual calendar custom celebrated at May Day and originally formed by chimney sweeps. Processions would have musicians, dancers, and other well-dressed participants, but the centrepiece would be a man carrying a wicker or basket-work frame which was covered with greenery and flowers. This was the Jack.

The earliest reference to the Jack in the Green seems to be from the eighteenth century, but many writers have suggested that the character comes from a direct association with Robin Hood, the wild man, and so on. Once again, as with Lady Raglan's conjecture, there is no real evidence to back up this idea.

Returning to the image of the foliate head that we find in so many of our churches, on roof bosses, rood screens, or carved in other places, we should note that there are three distinct types. In its truest sense, it is a head which is almost completely covered in leaves, appearing to peer out from behind them. The other two variations are the Disgorging Head, where vegetation appears to be coming from the mouth of the figure, and the Bloodsucker Head, which has vegetation coming from all of the facial features—eyes, nose, and mouth.

One of the very earliest examples of imagery, which is said by many to portray a green man, is that of a statue of Dionysus covered in leaves, which may be found in Naples and has been dated to circa 420 BC. We might think of Dionysus predominantly as the "god of sex and wine" (a business card which I'm sure many would be pleased to present), but his more common portrayal before this was as a lord of nature and agriculture, rather like the Pagan images of the Horned God.

There is a carved figure of the Greco-Roman Okeanos, who is closely linked to Dionysus, in Turkey, and it seems to be the case that a number of European carvings used this as a template. This might offer up a possible route for the image to spread from its early beginnings into Europe and the West. However, the Lebanese leaf mask example from the second century referred to earlier was on a temple to Bacchus, and the Indian example from the eighth century is one of the earliest disgorging heads. These examples seem to give credence to the notion that a similar image in different cultures formed in parallel and show that the route into Europe may be more complex.

We can see how the green man is such a powerful archetype that it moved between cultures and religions with little difficulty. The Christian Church certainly took on much of the imagery of Dionysus in the medieval period. Another possible influence that has been suggested is that the Church might have drawn on the "Cult of the Head." This refers to the importance of both the human head as the dwelling place of the soul, and tree worship, to the Celtic peoples. Combining these two images would give us something like a green man figure. So, does this feed into the image? It is hard to say for certain.

Having survived the Middle Ages, the Reformation, and the time of the Renaissance, the green man is once again being linked more with nature as the image spreads out from churches into other buildings, as well as in art and on both architectural embellishments and other carved items, such as furniture. As a symbol of nature and of regeneration, foliate heads are now often representative of conservation and our need to look after nature.

To come back to the idea of the wild man or man of the woods, the fifteenth-century carved font at St Catherine's Church in Ludham is unusual for the fact that, alongside images of the lion of St Mark, an eagle, and an angel are two woodwoses. Whoever carved this piece was clearly keeping their options open.

The woodwose is a mythical forest creature which the *Oxford English Dictionary* describes as a "wild man of the woods." This description is somewhat erroneous. Its inaccuracy comes not only from the fact that woodwoses do not just dwell among trees, at least in our medieval representations of them, but also because you can find female woodwoses as well as male ones.

The font at St Catherine's is particularly rare because it carries carvings of both a male and a female woodwose. Woodwose carvings seem to be particularly common in churches in the county of Suffolk, often in fonts, but also on roof bosses and in other areas. They are often depicted as battling with lions, or sometimes dragons, and, so, are probably being used as a signifier of protection from evil spirits or other threats.

Some woodwoses are depicted with clubs raised, and others with clubs pointing down. It has been suggested that the former is a depiction of a "'wild' woodwose," whereas the latter with the less-threatening-looking club has been converted to Christianity. There appears to be no evidence to back up this claim.

The Church of St Senara in the Cornish village of Zennor dates from 1150, although it is probable that there was a Celtic church on the same site from the sixth century onwards. The interior of St Senara's is notable for having one surviving medieval bench end. It was carved more than five centuries ago and is now known as the Mermaid Chair. The figure depicted is a mermaid with her tail folded to the side of her, holding a mirror in her right hand and a comb in her left. A well-known folk tale surrounds this chair. Folklorist William Bottrell collected a couple of different versions of the "Mermaid of Zennor" story in the 1870s.

The mermaid would come to church each Sunday to listen to the choir and to sing herself, and she would sit on what is now called the Mermaid Chair while she was there. Mathey Trewella, the son of the churchwarden and known as the best singer in the parish, became enamoured with the girl, and they ended up going away together. They were never seen on dry land again.

It was years later that the fate of Mathey, or Mathew as he is sometimes referred to as, was learned. The news was imparted to the captain of a ship who had anchored off nearby Pendower Cove by the very same mermaid, who had swum alongside the vessel. She told the captain that her name was Morveren and that she was one of the daughters of Llyr, the king of the ocean. She wanted to get back home to her children, she explained, but she couldn't because the anchor that the captain had dropped was blocking the entrance to her house. She, therefore, asked the captain if he would mind moving.

Although Morveren had been perfectly pleasant and civil, and given no cause for alarm, the captain was very well-aware from stories that mermaids were considered to be unlucky and so he quickly headed out to sea.

In another of the collected versions, Mathey and the mermaid fell in love in the church as soon as their eyes had met, but this had scared the mermaid. So, she fled, heading back to the sea. Mathey and several others of the congregation ran after her. Morveren tripped on her dress, which afforded the lad a glimpse of her fish tail (how she runs on this is never explained). Despite her protestations that she belonged in the water, Mathey followed, insisting, "I will go with ye. For with ye is where I belong."

He picked the mermaid up and ran with her into the sea, never to be seen again. However, according to this story, Mathey continued to sing from his new home in the water. If the conditions were good, then he would sing softly and high, but if Llyr was going to make the seas unfavourable, then his song would be deeper. By this means, the fishermen of the area would know when to go out on the water in pursuit of their catch and when to stow their boats in port and remain safely at home.

The story of the mermaid is somewhat unusual, in that most northern European merfolk and other water spirits would be turned away by Christian belief rather than being attracted to it. The story of the mermaid is undoubtedly later than the chair itself and was probably created based on the unusual carving in the church.

The earliest example of a mermaid in an English church may be that found in the Norman Chapel at Durham Castle. Another good example is found on a misericord in Carlisle Cathedral. The carving has long since lost one arm, with the traditional comb held in the hand, but the other hand does still hold a mirror. This particular example dates from the early 1400s.

A misericord is a small wooden shelf on the underside of a folding church seat. When the seat is folded up, it works as a sort of shelf against which a standing person may lean for a little additional comfort. The misericord came into use at the time that prayers said during the daily canonical hours such as Matins or Vespers had to be delivered whilst standing and lifting your hands towards Heaven. They are also sometimes called "mercy seats," after the gold lid with carved cherubim which sat on the Ark of the Covenant.

Many misericords featured objects which could be secular—sometimes Pagan, sometimes humorous, and sometimes lewd. After all, they were hidden for all of the time that the seat was folded down. There are many examples of foliate heads on mercy seats, alongside dragons, wyverns, and other animals from medieval bestiaries. An amusing example from Bristol Cathedral depicts a woman throwing a bowl at a man who is taking the lid from her cooking pot, presumably to steal some of the food she is making. There is a fine carving in Notre Dame cathedral of a man doubled over, looking through his legs, and parting his exposed buttocks—a kind of reflection of the sheela na gig in some respects. Buttock-flashing crops up a number of times on misericords.

Returning to the topic at hand, there are other examples of mermaids featured on mercy seats as well. St Lawrence Church in Ludlow has an example of a mermaid centred between two large fish-like creatures with rows of sharp teeth on either side. In exactly the same way as the one at Carlisle Cathedral, her hand holding a mirror is intact, but the arm which would have held the comb aloft is broken off at the elbow.

Folklore tells us that in many stories featuring merfolk from different parts of the world, the women are beautiful, whereas the mermen are ugly and monstrous. This is the reason that we often find stories of interbreeding between mermaids and human males, such as with the Mermaid of Zennor—mermen are not a good catch!

We may have here the explanation for why we find examples of the mermaid as an icon in Christian churches. When we consider the common use of folk tales in education, especially in Christianised forms as morality tales, it might be the case that these church examples are designed to serve as warnings against the dangers of desiring women for their beauty.

That being said, around the time of the fifteenth century when the Mermaid Chair is believed to have been carved, the symbol of the mermaid was also used to teach people about the dual nature of Christ—human and also divine. Merfolk were quite common in Cornish churches, at least at this time, but the representation of the Mermaid of Zennor is one of the few that survives today.

The Church of St Senara, home of the Mermaid Chair, has a circular graveyard which is an Iron Age site. It sits on top of older boundaries which date from the Stone Age and Bronze Age. Whilst the particular site has no megaliths or stones of note which date from this period, other churchyards most certainly do...and others might.

Falling into the latter category is St John's Church, in Ysbyty Cynfyn, Ceredigion in Wales. Some people believe that this church, which was built in 1827 in the same location as an earlier church on the site, was constructed inside a stone circle. The evidence cited for this are three large standing stones which are set into the southeastern part of the churchyard boundary wall. This is, however, somewhat debated, as there is no record of the stones being in their locations prior to 1833, which leads to speculation that they could be nothing more than a folly installed in that century. (A *folly* is an ornamental reconstruction of an old structure built to serve no particular purpose.)

There is no doubt about the example to be found at Midmar Parish Church in Aberdeenshire, however. The church here was built in 1787 to replace an earlier one which was located a short distance away at the foot of a hill and had been constructed alongside a Bronze Age recumbent stone circle. Measuring 17.3 metres in diameter, the Midmar stone circle is considered to be one of the best-preserved examples in Scotland. Many sources will tell you that the circle was "previously worshipped by Druids," but we should be well-aware by now of accepting these sorts of claims at face value.

Prominent in the promotion of ideas surrounding prehistoric structures and their links to Druidry was the antiquarian and clergyman Willian Stukeley, writing in the eighteenth century. At the time, he was considered to be an authority on the subject, although many of his ideas were not of his own devising and built on earlier ones. The concepts of longevity from primeval religions and ancient structures that he discussed gradually fell out of favour, being recognised as, for the most part, speculative, and are dismissed by many scholars today. However, a lasting legacy remains from this time of Druidic associations within both archaeology and folklore which will probably never go away.

One of the many ancient stones that William Stukeley examined is known as the Rudston Monolith. It stands in the churchyard of All Saints' Church, Rudston in the East Riding of Yorkshire, approximately twelve feet from the northeast corner of the church. The building, of which only the lower part of the tower and font are now original, was constructed around AD 1100 by Lord of the Manor, William Peverel.

At eight metres in height and approximately two in width, the Rudston monolith is the tallest prehistoric standing stone to be found in Britain. When the Christian church was built in Rudston, the stone had already been in place for at least three thousand years. It was probably quarried a few miles away and transported to where it stands, although it is also possible that it may be a large glacial erratic.

The corner of the churchyard also houses a small stone which may be from a local barrow and the remains of a cist that were removed from another barrow in the late nineteenth century and brought to the site.

Stukeley believed that the visible part of the Rudston Monolith was only half of its full size. He also claimed to have found human remains near the stone which, in his opinion, showed that it had been a place of human sacrifice. Again, this is pure speculation. The number of nearby barrows and the general landscape of the area would suggest that a number of burials could have been made there, and there are no records of any tangible signs of injury that would point to sacrifice.

With many out-of-place objects in the landscape, folklore has arisen to explain how they came to be there, and the Rudston Monolith in no exception. In this case, there are a couple of different legendary explanations. One says that the stone was dropped from above, presumably by a vengeful God, where it killed a group of people who were desecrating the churchyard. This, of course, makes no sense, as the churchyard is associated with the twelfth-century church, and yet the stone had already been there for three millennia at that point. Maybe God picked it up and dropped it again?

It is possible that this story developed out of an actual event which took place in the village of Wold Newton, which lies about six miles distant of Rudston. On 13 December 1795, ploughman John Shipley was outside when a twenty-five-kilogram stone fell from the sky, narrowly missing him. It hit the ground, displacing a foot of soil, before embedding itself in the chalk beneath. Later analysis showed this to be a meteorite. It was displayed in London by the man who owned the land on which it fell, Major Edward Topham, and can still be viewed in the city today at the Natural History Museum. We saw an example of a church being struck by a meteorite in the first chapter.

The second piece of folklore at Rudston suggests that the stone was thrown by the Devil in an attempt to destroy the church, but that God deflected it, and it fell in the current location. Once again, God's hand is involved, and, once again, there is no consideration for the three thousand years that it had already been there. God might be omnipresent, but does he have a TARDIS? Folklore never lets the facts get in the way of a good tale, of course.

There are similar stories to be found at many other churches. St Twrog's Church at Maentwrog in the Welsh county of Gwynedd has a standing stone close to the belfry door which shares its name with the location of the church—Maen Twrog. In the Welsh language, *maen* means "stone." St Twrog, who founded the church on this site in the sixth century, was said to have thrown this stone from a nearby mountain, Moelwyn, in order to crush a Pagan altar that was built where the church now stands. Markings still visible on the stone are, according to the story, the remains of the saint's handprints.

Stones thrown by the Devil or other legendary characters are a common trope in folklore and grow out of earlier stories from the time when giants were said to roam the earth in many cases. In Chapter Six, we will look at the Devil in more detail. That is, after all, where he lives…in the detail.

Some people have suggested that the place name, Rudston, translates as "cross stone," from the word *rood,* the life-sized crucifix which is displayed in the central axis of a church. But we need to be very cautious about making leaps of faith when we examine the etymology behind place names. We know that the name "Rudston" is in existence in 1086 because it is listed as such in the Domesday Book. We also know that the church was built in the twelfth century, but we don't have evidence of another Christian church on this site before that. So, the "rood stone" translation would have to exist before the church was built.

There is a possible alternative. The word *rud* comes from an Old Norse term for "pasture, or another similar clearing." This would make the meaning of Rudstone "stone in the clearing," which seems more logical.

Actual carved stone crosses used to be very common across the English landscape. Many still remain, although their numbers are much smaller now, and some examples are fragmentary after years of erosion or other damage. Whilst much of the embellishment on these crosses is of Christian imagery, it is not unusual to find a mix of Christian and Pagan iconography. Some high church crosses also feature Anglo-Saxon runic carvings.

One such Saxon stone cross, dating to the seventh century, stands in the churchyard of St Lawrence's in the Derbyshire village of Eyam, known historically for locking itself down in voluntary quarantine to avoid spreading the plague elsewhere. Whilst this cross has a number of religious symbols on its arms and shaft—including a Virgin and Child, figures with trumpets, and others with crosses—the sides are covered with runes and Scandinavian knots.

This knot is made up of a set of three interlocked triangles, which is symbolic of the cycle of life and death. We might compare this with the imagery surrounding the triskele in churches that we explored earlier.

A similar cross can be found in the churchyard at Gosforth, in Cumbria. Being close to the border with Scotland, this is an area which would have seen much incursion by Scandinavians in its early history, and this cross is good testament to that. Made of red sandstone, the cross is particularly tall, at almost 4.5 metres, and dates back over a thousand years. It is covered with Anglo-Scandinavian carvings which, again, are a mix of Christian religious and Pagan images. Depictions of Christ at the time of crucifixion sit alongside representations of Loki, Thor, and Odin.

A similar mix of images can be found inside the church also. There is a good example of a Viking hogback tombstone which shows Thor fishing for the Midgard Serpent, for instance.

Across the Irish Sea in County Wickland, St Kevin's Cross stands in Glendalough graveyard. Carved from a single piece of granite, the cross stands at a height of around 2.5 metres with arms of over a metre.

The cross takes the form of what we now generally term a Celtic cross, being made up of a standard Christian cross which features a circular halo, or nimbus, around its intersection point. Ringed crosses of this style emerged in the Middle Ages and became widespread over a period of three hundred years up to the twelfth century.

The origins of this cross are not known for certain, but it is highly likely that it either derives from, or is related to, the much earlier solar, sun, or wheel cross, which is an equilateral cross seated inside a circle. Sun crosses are a staple of prehistoric symbolic art from the Neolithic to the Bronze Age.

Celtic crosses received a massive boost from the nineteenth century onwards, thanks to the Celtic Revival, and are frequently featured in artwork, especially on pewter jewellery.

Irish legend states that the Christian cross was introduced by St Patrick, and that he combined this with the solar cross in order help to demonstrate the power of the Christian symbol to Pagan sun worshippers. There is little evidence for this, but the story persists and is ascribed to St Kevin's cross as well. Another piece of local folklore attached to this cross says that if you can wrap your arms around the entire body of the cross and touch your fingertips together, then your wishes will be granted. Such is the power of having arms like an orangutan, evidently.

Other debate surrounds St Patrick, with regard to his portrayal in Ireland as the slayer of two serpent gods named Corra and Caoranach, mainly because snakes are not commonly found as an animal in the country. There are obvious parallels with the famous story of St George and the Dragon, considered so quintessentially English despite the fact that George was a Turkish knight and also St Michael. Michael acts as a dragon slayer in folklore from England and Scotland. In many of these stories, the suggestion is that the first represents Christianity overcoming the earlier Pagan influences. A number of churches contain carvings of St Michael and a dragon, such as on a door lintel above the north transept at Southwell Minster.

These standing stones and megaliths might put us in mind of the number of obelisks which might be found in churchyards. Obelisks, like Celtic crosses, became quite widespread as part of the Revival movements.

Some cite the influence of freemasonry on the introduction of significant numbers of obelisks, but, although there are undoubtedly influences to be found in cemetery art from the masons, they do not have that much responsibility for the prevalence of the obelisk. This has more to do with Egyptian influences.

The Napoleonic campaigns in Egypt at the turn of the nineteenth century, coupled with the rising numbers of archaeological digs in the country and the major discoveries of tombs such as Tutankhamun's, captured the public's imagination, and Egyptian symbolism, art, and architecture began to find its way into public spaces in the United Kingdom and America. Obelisks were perfectly suited to burial sites such as churchyards and cemeteries. They had a small footprint, and yet were imposing and grand. They had clean artistic lines and were significantly cheaper than statues or mausoleums.

The name "mausoleum" finds its origin in what is now Turkey. When King Mausolos died, somewhere around 350 BC, his widow ordered a particularly impressive tomb to be built for his remains. This tomb, at Halicarnassus, became one of the seven wonders of the ancient world.

A further Egyptian link with Christian churches can be found with the symbol of the Ankh, a cross with a loop on the top. The Ankh is a symbol of life and immortality, with a secondary reading of death and rebirth. It is found widely in Egyptian hieroglyphics and tomb adornments, carried by gods, nobles, and leaders.

The shape of the Ankh symbolised a fusion of God and Goddess, and this is perhaps one of the reasons why it was adopted as a useful symbol in Wiccan practices later. It provided protection on the spiritual journey after death. Early Coptic Christians also took on the symbol of the Ankh as an alternative version of the cross, and we can find many examples appearing in carvings in Coptic churches. Perhaps it isn't too far of a stretch to envisage some similarities between the Ankh and the solar cross and everything in terms of what the symbols both represent. Both are comprised of a cross and either a circle or loop, which, in both cases, is thought to be symbolic of the sun. The combination of cross and circle is perhaps something of an archetypal image.

Another image particularly linked with the Christian church, but which probably has earlier roots, is the *ichthys,* made up of two intersecting arcs which, together, suggest the shape of a fish. The name *ichthys* has a dual meaning. It is the Greek word for "fish," which the symbol represents, but is also formed by an acrostic of the Greek words which make up the phrase *Iēsous Christos, Theou Yios, Sōtēr,* meaning "Jesus Christ, Son of God, Saviour" in English.

This all sounds very secretive, and there might be good reason for that, as it has been suggested that the symbol was used for believers in the Christian faith to make themselves known to each other during times of persecution from Rome.

The first mention that we can find of the ichthys as a Christian symbol comes from approximately two hundred years after the birth of Christ. Clement of Alexandria issued a proclamation to Christians at this time to use images of either fish or doves on the rings that they used to make wax seals.

It is the two-part nature of the symbol which has led people to believe that it was a sort of test to see whether the person who you met was also of the Christian faith, a little like the "secret handshake" of the freemasons. You would draw one of the arcs of the symbol, perhaps in the dirt on the ground, and then if the other person shared your faith, they would show this by drawing the other half. There is no definite evidence that this is the case, but it is certainly possible.

However, we do need to make allowance for the fact that we find symbolism relating to fishes from outside of the Christian faith, and much earlier. The Egyptian cult of Isis used a fish symbol as part of their devotion. This travelled back to Ancient Greece and Rome following Alexander the Great's conquest of Egypt in the third century BC, where it became subsumed into Pagan rituals, being representative of fertility.

An obvious architectural influence from Egypt which is more unusual than the obelisks, and yet, has still found its way into some of our churchyards is the pyramid. There are a few examples of pyramid tombs, usually constructed for notable individuals. As with standings stones or other features which are out of the ordinary, these structures will usually be accompanied by tales of folklore which have grown up around them.

Take, for example, the churchyard outside St Thomas Becket Church at Brightling in Surrey, which dates from the twelfth century and has probably been rededicated to Becket from an early name, due to its inclusion in the Domesday Book.

In a pyramid tomb here is buried the body of nineteenth-century conservative member of parliament, John Fuller, who was also known as "Mad Jack." He was known to be a drunkard and an eccentric, and his behaviour in the House of Commons was so poor that he was threatened with time in prison if he did not clean up his act.

There are a number of follies in the landscape around the Brightling area which are down to Fuller and his drunken wagers. The Sugar Life is a structure near Wood's Corner which resembles a church spire. One night, Fuller bet a friend that he could see the spire of Dallington Church from his house. When it turned out that, in fact, he couldn't see it at all, he had the folly built just to prove himself right.

Mad Jack was also responsible for the construction of a tower in the middle of a field, an obelisk on the top of Brightling Down, and a Greek-style temple in the grounds of Brightling Park. It is not clear why he built any of them.

He planned the pyramid-shaped resting place for himself prior to his death in 1834. If local folklore was to be believed, then he was interred sitting at a table, on which was laid out a roast chicken and a bottle of port, and that the floor of the tomb was covered in broken glass in order to prevent the Devil from taking his soul. In 1982, renovation work was undertaken on the pyramid. None of these things proved to be true.

Another man who was said to have been buried sitting down, again in a pyramid, was engineer William Mackenzie. He had amassed a fortune with his work on the railways, both in the United Kingdom and Europe, and, when he died in 1851, his estate passed to his brother Edward. To begin with, Edward had his brother buried with his first wife, and then, when his second wife died in 1867, he had her body laid with the pair of them. A year later, in 1868, he commissioned a fifteen-foot-high granite pyramid to be built over the top of the graves. Nobody knows why, but presumably it tied in with the Victorian interest in Egyptology alluded to earlier.

William Mackenzie was, allegedly, a keen gambler, and folklore tells that he was buried sitting on a chair, holding a hand of cards. The reason for this surrounds the idea that his money and skill engineering had come about through a bargain with the Devil. The terms of this deal were that the Devil would be able to claim Mackenzie's soul if he ever trumped his cards. The burial and the cards chosen to ensure that this can never happen.

Once again, sadly, there is no truth in the folkloric story, as we know that the interment is in a vault, and they don't tend to allow for chairs. There are also reports of William Mackenzie's ghost walking in the area, dressed in a top hat and cape.

There are a number of churchyard pyramid tombs, but none of them are quite on the scale of the proposal put forward in the nineteenth century by London architect Thomas Willson to build a giant pyramid mortuary in the city. If it had gone ahead, this would have taken shape in the 1830s as a solution to the volume of bodies from the city that needed disposal.

Willson submitted plans for a pyramid of such scale that its base would have covered eighteen acres, and its height would have reached ninety-four stories. By contrast, the Great Pyramid is around half this height, and its 598,000 square feet of base cover 13.5 acres.

In the end, the pyramid was never built and, instead, the city authorities decided to create the garden cemeteries that we know today. It was probably the right choice.

CHAPTER FIVE

MAGIC AND WITCHCRAFT IN THE CHURCHYARD

PERHAPS NOT UNSURPRISINGLY for someone who spends a lot of time working with folkloric topics, I know a lot of people connected with different forms of what might come under the umbrella term of "Witchcraft." Some of them have a passing interest, some study the subject from different perspectives, some just like the aesthetic, and some are practitioners.

From the latter, I will occasionally see comments posted on social media or overheard in conversation, along the lines of "going to be a late night tonight—popping up to the graveyard at midnight to restock my dirt."

In folk magic, the use of soil from a cemetery or graveyard has a long history across many cultures. There are suggestions from ancient Egyptian texts that it was used ritually, and it is widely used in Southern magical practices, such as Hoodoo, where "goofer dirt" refers to earth which has been removed from the grave of someone who was either considered to be powerful in some way or died under circumstances which would be considered to increase the power of a spell being undertaken.

To some, the use of earth from a gravesite might seem disrespectful. However, to the practitioner, nothing could be further from the truth. Only small amounts are collected, and always with the utmost reverence, with offerings being required in return. To those who use it, there is far more disrespect shown to the spirits of the dead by individuals who sell any old earth under the label of "graveyard dirt." This is the reason that most people who undertake magical workings will collect their own.

Perhaps slightly less respectful is the story of a woman from Strathavon in Scotland whose cattle succumbed to a disease which was rampant in the area at the time. Having tried all the usual cures with no success, she came to believe that they must have been bewitched. In order to undo this supernatural problem, she would need to use a tried-and-tested curative, which is described in the anonymously written 1889 book *Folk-lore and Legends, Scotland* as "the juice of a dead head from the churchyard."

Not being difficult enough to procure, it was vital that this item was exhumed at the hour of midnight. The woman proceeded to the churchyard and found a suitable grave, but upon extracting a skull, a spectral voice was heard to proclaim, "that is my head; let it alone." The woman returned the skull and took up another from the same plot, but the voice returned and exclaimed, "that is my father's head." The same happened again with two more skulls—the grandfather and grandmother—from what was, evidently, a family grave.

In the end, the woman struck a bargain with the spirit, explaining her predicament, and it was agreed that the grandfather's skull could be taken and used, as long as it was returned to the grave by cock crow. This the woman did and, according to the story, her cattle did indeed recover.

Over time, there has been a constantly shifting dynamic between the Church and folk magic. This is far from being as simplistic as the two being generally mutually exclusive. It also goes beyond the more formal Christian religion frowning on or condoning the other. Depending on your point of view, biblical miracles are as magical and superstitious as anything conjured as part of folk magic practices. Playing devil's advocate and removing any kind of faith or belief system, is there such a big difference between the Resurrection story and ghosts witnessed in church buildings?

The adoption and combining of older festival and celebration times with the Christian calendar has obviously fed into this dynamic. For example, consider the number of celebrations which surround harvest time. Vestiges of older customs—such as Crying the Neck, a harvest tradition where the first cut corn is held up to be celebrated through a series of calls and responses—sits alongside church services, such as the blessing of the plough and harvest festivals.

Pagan celebrations mark the start of the harvest season through Lughnasadh, traditionally held on the first of August, which sits roughly midway between the summer solstice and the autumn equinox. Christian celebrations use *Lammas,* from the Old English meaning "loaf-mass," also on August 1. Both seek to celebrate the crops and hope to ensure that there will be a good and bountiful harvest. Historically, the lead up to harvest time was a period in which communities could suffer from a lack of food, leading to malnutrition or worse. With harvest came hope for enough stocks of food to see people through the difficult winter months.

Interestingly, this is also a time that shows that the process of adopting other people's religious ideas into your own is not a one-way practice—in other words, it is not always the Christian Church subsuming Pagan rituals into their own. Modern Pagans have adopted the term Lammas alongside Lughnasadh, with the two often being used interchangeably in different artistic renderings of the "Wheel of the Year" concept.

The observation that all of this leads to is that there are many connections between the Church, or Christian religion, and magic. It is a pervading myth that cunning folk, village witches, and healers were uneducated and always illiterate. Most certainly had a good working knowledge of the Bible and considered that their skills sat alongside the church. Sometimes, members of the clergy would seek advice from these practitioners, using the services on one hand that, with the other, they were expected to be decrying in their sermon on a Sunday.

If you open any good book of spells and charms, the chances are high that you will turn to one that invokes biblical characters or uses a psalm as part of its construction. To test my own theory, I reached down for a copy from my own shelves of *The British Book of Spells and Charms,* compiled by Graham King, past owner of the Museum of Witchcraft and Magic in Boscastle, Cornwall. I opened the book randomly to a charm to offer protected sleep at night:

Matthew, Mark, Luke, and John,
Bless the bed that I lie on;
There are four corners to my bed,
And four angels overspread,
Two at the feet, two at the head.
If any ill thing be betide,
Beneath your wings my body hide.
Matthew, Mark, Luke and John
Bless the bed that I lie on. Amen.

This charm was collected from Lancashire and published in John Harland and Thomas Turner Wilkinson's *Lancashire Folk-lore* in 1882, although it is much older than this. In 1656, Thomas Ady published *A Candle in the Dark* which he described as: "A treatise concerning the nature of witches and witchcraft: being advice to judges, sheriffs, justices of the peace, and grand jury-men*[sic]*, what to do, before they passe sentence on such as are arraigned for their lives as witches." In the seventeenth century, the titles were often as long as the publications that followed. Ady refers to "an old woman in Essex" who he says every night, when she lay down to sleep, would say:

Matthew, Mark, Luke and John,
The Bed be Blessed that I lye on.

He described this as a "Popish Charm," but the origins of the charm, which is generally known as the "Black Paternoster," are probably Babylonian.

However, interestingly, there are rituals in other practices that have similarities, such as invoking the Archangels at cardinal points. Modern Wiccan rituals often begin by "calling the quarters," which is not so far removed. Irish midwives would describe a cross in the air at the four corners of a house in which a woman was birthing, whilst also using a variation of the verse which ended:

New Moon, New Moon, God bless me
God bless this house and family.

It is easy to dismiss such charms as culturally outdated, but, because of its age and rhyming structure, the Black Paternoster is still used to this day in ever more unusual ways. A representative of the Gwynedd Mercy University softball team in Pennsylvania posted a tweet before a game on 1 October 2013 which read:

Matthew, Mark, Luke and John
Bless this field we play upon.
If we do our very best,
God will help us do the rest.

Gwynedd Mercy is a private Roman Catholic university founded in 1948 as a junior college by the Sisters of Mercy—that is, the women's religious institute in the Roman Catholic Church, not the British Gothic rock band…just to avoid any misunderstanding later!

The Paternoster also features in a children's playground rhyme:

Matthew, Mark, Luke and John
Went to bed with their britches on
John got up in the middle of the night
And said his britches were too tight.

This, in turn, is possibly a conflation with the eighteenth-century nursery rhyme which begins, "diddle, diddle, dumpling, my son John, went to bed with his trousers on." At this point, things start to get complicated, and we stray from the point. Many charms are a mix of beliefs and, therefore, could be deconstructed in the same way.

As well as being known for consulting folk magic practitioners, a number of clergymen were believed to have particular skills of their own. In English folklore, these have become known as "conjuring parsons," and stories of their deeds suggest a range of skillsets, from the probably accurate to the almost certainly legendary.

Falling into the former category was a parson named Harris who lived and served in the Dartmoor village and parish of Hennock. He developed a reputation of being able to identify thieves through divination. In most cases, his techniques had little to do with magic and everything to do with psychology. Once, after a farmer came to consult with the parson about the theft of three of his geese, Harris assured the man that the thief would be identified and shamed. Sure enough, in church the following Sunday, parson Harris declared to the congregation that he had consulted his books and drawn his figures, and that he had conjured a spell to cause three feathers from the stolen geese to immediately stick to the nose of the thief. As he spoke, a man in the congregation instinctively brushed his nose, apparently revealing his guilt. What is more interesting here is not the professed "magical" ability (there really isn't any), but rather the fact that the villagers held the belief that the parson used it.

Other clergymen were thought to have more occult knowledge, which they gleaned from their personal libraries of magical tomes. One of these, William Gimmingham, who was the rector at the Church in the Devon town of Bratton Fleming in the early nineteenth century, was said to have had to intervene when his servants accidentally conjured up a number of fowl in his house by reading one of his books while he was in church. However, a very similar story has been told of other vicars, and, ultimately, is really just a retelling of the plot of *The Sorcerer's Apprentice.*

Such stories in folklore usually come about through the process of "othering" individuals, as we frequently see with witches. It happens with people of highly skilled trades, such as the blacksmith or the weaver, who must have made a deal with a higher power to receive their knowledge. It happens with those who hold power or wealth in a community—through resentment of them by the general population or because they abuse their position—and with people who are unusually eccentric, which William Gimmingham apparently was.

Such associations were often made after the death of the person, rather than during their lifetime, for fear of repercussions. Such is the case at one of the earliest recorded nunneries in Ireland.

Monasternagalliagduff, also known as the Abbey of St Catherine de O'Conyl or St Katherine's Abbey, was an Augustinian abbey in County Limerick, Ireland, whose remains lie in a valley near Shanagolden. The church on the site dated to the thirteenth century (with later modifications), and it appears that there was associated land for burials there too.

The abbey's name in Irish is *Mainistir nag Cailleach Dubh,* which means "The Black Nuns' Abbey." This hints at some confusion which might have led to a part of the folklore here.

The fate of the abbey perhaps came from a couple of different directions. It was officially decommissioned in 1541 as part of the Irish Reformation and the Dissolution of the Monasteries. However, folklore in the area records that, prior to that, an order was issued in 1432 by Pope Martin V to cease the day-to-day functions of the abbey, because there had been allegations made against the abbess for black Witchcraft and debauched acts.

Two small rooms can be seen in the present-day ruins of the abbey. One of these was the sacristy, but it has become known as the "Black Hag's Cell." It was claimed that the abbess practiced her Witchcraft in this room (as well as engaging in some unusual sexual acts).

While there is no evidence that either of these things took place, the stories possibly arose and were spread as propaganda at the time of the Dissolution in an effort to prove the validity of the closure. It was said that the abbess remained alone at the site when all of the sisters left. Poisoned by her own black magic, the legend says that, as the building crumbled away, she too withered and her skin gradually blackened.

It is a suitably florid and impressive idea for a folk tale. In fact, the name "Black Hag's Cell" most likely arises from a misunderstanding of the translation of the Irish *cailleach dhubh,* which is the Old Irish for "black nun." Many sources today mistakenly name the site at "The Black Hag's Abbey" rather than the correct translation.

There are, naturally, plenty of folkloric stories to connect witches to churches and their grounds in different ways.

The parish church of St Nicholas in the Essex village of Canewdon dates from the fourteenth century and overlooks the River Crouch from an elevated position on a nearby hill. It has a sizeable tower, which can be seen from miles around. Its erection was said to have come about in celebration of the victory at the Battle of Agincourt by King Henry V.

The village of Canewdon has been connected with Witchcraft for a long time, and some of these connections reference the Church. Folklore tells us that six witches will always remain here. If a stone falls from the church tower, this signifies that one of the witches has died, but another has taken her place.

Essex is notable in the history of Witchcraft because it was the main operating area of the self-styled "Witchfinder General" Matthew Hopkins. Despite this, the historical record shows that only three women were tried at Canewdon. This has led people to speculate that such was the fear of witches in the area that even Matthew Hopkins avoided the place. It has probably fed into the reputation of the village being "the most haunted in England," along with Pluckley, Borley, and about a gazillion other places.

Aside from the superstitious belief surrounding the church tower and some other rituals connected with the churchyard which we will return to shortly, most of the ties with Witchcraft seem to have been retrospectively mapped onto the location because of claims surrounding one cunning man, George Pickingill.

Pickingill worked as a farm labourer in Canewdon, but was also widely reported to have been consulted for folk remedies to cure illnesses or find lost items. He was not particularly known of outside of the East Essex area until the intervention of two other people in the 1960s and 1970s.

The first of these was folklorist and author Eric Maple, who made a particular study of Witchcraft that was reported in the county of Essex between the late nineteenth and early twentieth centuries. His articles on witches from Essex have been praised for being good field research written up without the need for jargon or over-analysis. However, at the same time, some have suggested that the people who Maple collected from were actually telling stories concerning another folk magician from the area, James Murrell, or relating other stories to keep him happy. Evidence does seem to suggest that some of the events attributed to Pinkingill are accurate, however.

Second, and probably more influential in terms of propagating the Witchcraft connections, was an occultist named Bill Liddell. Writing in the 1970s, Liddell published an account claiming that Pickingill was part of a hereditary witch cult, from which he ran a coven in Canewdon, and was instrumental in the formation of nine others across the South of England. This information, according to Liddell, was given to him by members of other secret witch families in the area—perhaps, the ones for whom the stones of the church tower occasionally fell.

The witch-cult hypothesis, which suggests that those put on trial as witches in early modern England were followers of suppressed Pagan religious beliefs that continued throughout Christianisation, has been roundly dismissed by most academics and historians alike. Liddell's further claims that

Pickingill reformed the witch-cult and, therefore, essentially created the structure which would be adopted as Gardnerian Wicca have been similarly criticised by practitioners such as Doreen Valiente.

Suggestions have been made that the Church of St Nicholas was the meeting ground of the Canewdon coven. As you might expect, this has led to it becoming an attractive site for legend trippers and paranormal investigators. In the final chapter, we will see an example of these sorts of visits taken to extremes. To try and prevent problems in Canewdon, police apparently used to cordon off the church at Halloween.

The Church of St Michael and All Angels' in Edmondthorpe, Leicestershire, is an impressive church with a thirteenth-century crenelated tower. Unusually, an upper portion of the main church, added in the fifteenth century, is built with very different stone.

A monument inside of this church draws directly from one of the most significant tropes coming from stories of witches—the ability to shapeshift into an animal.

The monument is made of alabaster and is constructed over three tiers. It is the memorial of Sir Roger Smith, who died in 1655, and includes the effigies of his two wives. One of these, Lady Ann Smith, is the unfortunate individual who is now forever known as the "Witch of Edmondthorpe."

This attribution has come about because of nothing more than the fact that, due to a flaw in the alabaster that was sculpted for this effigy, the left wrist has a red discolouration, some of which extends across the folds of Lady Ann's dress.

The associated tale that has arisen is a variation whereby a farmer shoots and injures a hare, which turns out to be a witch running in the shape of the animal. Edmonton Hall, which was built by Sir Roger in 1621, was home to a white cat (black in some versions) which was something of a thief. On one occasion, the butler at the hall cornered the cat in the kitchen and attempted to dispatch it with a meat cleaver. The animal got away and never returned, but, in the process, its paw was wounded. Later the same day, Lady Ann was seen wearing a bandage around her wrist which, when removed, revealed a red scar.

There is no historic evidence that suggests that Lady Ann Smith was a witch, or even that she had any dealings with anyone who was said to be one. The story has grown purely from the flawed alabaster. But, over time, it has developed and taken on many other aspects. The monument is said to bleed under certain circumstances, but, of course, the circumstances alluded to are not mentioned.

The legend also states that the stain made by the cat's blood as it fled remained for centuries afterwards and could not be cleaned off. In 1920, then owner of Edmondthorpe Hall, Lady Yarborough, had the flagstones removed, and they were allegedly put on show in Gollings Workshop in nearby Wymondham. Unfortunately, Gollings builders, who perhaps worked on the hall at this time, no longer exist, and their buildings have now collapsed, so this part of the story cannot be corroborated.

The folklore surrounding Lady Ann ended up feeding into a real-life event during the Second World War. At this time, the hall was used as a depot for the storage of fuel for the military, but, in February of 1942, the mishandling of hot ashes from a coal fire sparked a blaze which would go on to destroy the building. However, the legendary version is a little different.

This tells that the hall was a camp used to house prisoners of war. This part is true, as they were accommodated in the nineteenth-century stable buildings. However, in this version, the fire was said to have started when a candle fell into a pot of fat. The candle was knocked into the pot because the cook threw a rolling pin across the kitchen at a cat that kept coming in trying to steal food. The cat was never seen again.

Aside from the collection of grave soil with which we opened this chapter, the churchyard may be home to other forms of magical practice or ritual. Circling the church a particular number of times, usually anticlockwise or widdershins, was common in some of these. The witches at Canewdon were said to have needed to circle the Church of St Nicholas in order to access certain powers. However, it was also said that if you did so at midnight, or on Halloween, then you might see the Devil, or be forced to dance with the witches themselves. Some even believed that the act would open a portal which could transport you to another place and time.

Sweden has a unique walking ritual which was said to be able to assist an individual in divining the future. Known in the Swedish language as *årsgång,* translating as "year walk," the divination practice is recorded back to the sixteen hundred, but may be earlier. Typically, the year walk would be performed on either Christmas Eve, or, more usually, New Year's Eve—liminal holiday times which were seen much as Halloween is now in terms of being a time at which it was easier to commune with spirits.

The ritual began with a day confined in a dark room, alone with nothing to eat or drink. As midnight struck, the walker would leave the room and set out for their local church. On the walk through the forests and countryside, they would come across many supernatural creatures from Swedish folklore, who would try and prevent the walker from reaching the church, whilst still obeying the rules of the ritual.

The year walk was a solitary practice, and it was forbidden to communicate with anyone else. There could be dire consequences if the person undertaking the walk failed to remain silent and solemn throughout. Sometimes, the supernatural creatures that the walker had to contend with might use more unconventional means than instilling terror in order to try and obstruct the walk.

Swedish folklorist Tommy Kuusela found an account in the Folklore Archives at Uppsala University which detailed a walker who came across some rats pulling along a hay cart. As the walker watched, one of the rats slipped on the icy ground and fell over, at the same time "farting so loudly that it could be heard across the whole parish." This caused the walker to burst out laughing, at which point the supernatural vision faded away, having served its purpose in bringing that particular year walk to an end.

Once reaching the church that they were aiming for, assuming that they had managed to circumvent the supernatural creatures which were trying to prevent them from doing so, the year walker would be required to walk around the building in a particular pattern. There are a number of different patterns described, from a number of circles to more complex examples.

The walker would now be able to learn certain information about the year ahead. This might be done by visiting new graves, some of which might have the sound of songs coming from them, or they might see spirits walking through the churchyard. By looking through the keyhole of the church door, other visions might reveal themselves to the walker.

The year walk might be undertaken to try and ascertain who might marry in the year ahead, whether there might be war or famine, good or bad crops expected, or, most often, who was likely to die in the coming year.

These techniques of circling the church or looking through the keyhole are far from unique in folklore terms, and we find them in many divination rituals involving the churchyard. For example, circling a church the magical number of seven times on a night with a full moon and then looking through the keyhole was said to summon the Devil. Whistling through the keyhole or pushing a pin through into the church would have the same effect.

If you wanted to see a vision of your future love, then Midsummer Eve was a good time to visit. As the church clock struck midnight, one would circle the church, scattering rosemary and rose leaves, whilst reciting:

> *"Rose leaves, rose leaves, rose leaves I strew,*
> *He that will love me, come after me now."*

The most well-known rituals in the churchyard are the ones that involve trying to get prior knowledge of who is going to die in the next twelve months. We will examine this subject in more detail in Chapter Seven, when we look at church-based superstitions.

A specific foretelling of death which comes to us from Welsh folklore is the corpse candle. Known in the native language as the *Canwyll Corph* or *Canwyllau Cryff*, the corpse candle probably comes from the same folkloric roots as will-o-the-wisps or other "earth light" phenomena. The lights were often seen on the lych ways, or corpse roads, which were used to carry bodies from the surrounding areas to the lych gate of the church, as we explored earlier in this book.

We find references to corpse candles from Welsh sources of the eighteenth and nineteenth centuries. Sometimes, they might be seen coming from a particular location which would make it obvious which family the death would be connected to, but there was also a system of interpretation of the light's appearance which helped to describe who the future deceased would be. A short-looking light, or candle, signify a young life, whereas a longer light would represent an older person. So, if two candles appeared together, one longer than the other, then it was likely that a parent and child would be about to die. The colour of the light would foretell the gender: red for a man and white for a woman.

An oral history recorded in 1979, now available from the National Museum of Wales to hear in the original Welsh or read in translated form, tells of one family's reminiscences about corpse candles. Mary Thomas describes the experiences of her grandfather:

> *He'd had many experiences of the corpse candle. My grandmother died when my mother was eight years old, my Uncle David six and Aunty Charlotte a baby, a young girl, twenty-eight years old. She died of the dicâd (tuberculosis), as they called it in those days, [and] there was no cure. And the night before she died he was by her bedside, and he saw a little lighted candle on the bed, and he saw it going out of the house. And then his wife died. And he saw his wife's corpse candle going out of*

the house. And she saw it too. She said: 'Do you see that light going out through the door, Tomos?' Both she and he saw the light, and she died the next day.

It was not only the bodies of the deceased that would be buried in churchyards. Sometimes, other objects would be buried as well, often for more magical purposes.

Readers will undoubtedly be aware of the use of witch bottles as a form of magical house protection. Coming from sometime around the seventeenth century, as far as we know, stone bottles known as "bellarmines" —then, later, glass bottles—would be filled with suitable materials before being buried under the floor or concealed in the wall of a property. Sharp objects would be combined with urine and sometimes human hair (ideally taken from the person who was believed to be a witch).

Whilst they were usually placed in private homes, farms, or business properties, there was an unusual find recorded in 1900 at St George's Church in the North Devon village of Monkleigh. St George's is an early fifteenth-century church, looking not unlike the (fictional) church on the cover of this book.

The find came about because the sexton at the time was exhuming a grave to carry out some ongoing work. About a foot into the soil, he unearthed a glass bottle, stopped with a cork stuck with pins and containing some form of inky fluid. Church procedures dictated that anything exhumed from a grave being worked on must be put back, which the sexton did as soon as he was able—but not before a number of people had examined it.

Amongst those who examined the bottle, which, for all intents and purposes, resembled a witch bottle, was the vicar at the time, Reverend L. Coutier Bigg. He was of the opinion that the bottle had once been used as a means of magical attack on somebody, and that that person had buried it in the churchyard in order to transfer the spell to the deceased.

This is unlikely to be the case, as this was not the way in which bottles such as this were generally used. There is plenty of folklore which does involve the transference of things from one place to another, such as disease or ill-wishing, but the bottle is not likely to have been used for this sort of spell.

Whilst the transfer of something ill is unlikely in this case, disease and illness—whether brought about by supernatural attack or by more normal biological methods—can find possible magical assistance in the churchyard. We have touched on the topic of holy wells already at the beginning of this book, and there are many of these closely associated with church ground which are said to have healing properties. Whether the origin of these healing attributes is Christian or pre-Christian is a topic that will often be up for debate.

The folk stories lying behind the establishment of many healing wells are often very similar. A saint, or some other notable individual, is attacked or murdered. Often, there is a miraculous happening, such as the person being beheaded and then reattaching his head (although, sometimes, he stays dead). Afterwards, the water that flows in the location takes on magical (or miraculous, depending on your approach to the topic) properties.

Such is the case with the well at the St Issui's Church in the Welsh village of Partrishow. More the size of a chapel, though with the status of a parish church, the building dates from the fourteenth century and has a particularly notable rood screen surviving from the year 1500. This still has its original loft, an intricately carved piece of woodwork that bears a fire breathing dragon alongside the more usual representations of the saints.

The Welsh saint, Issui, lived as a hermit by the well, which could be found on land next to the church in the sixth century. The well, fed from a stream flowing nearby, was originally just the place from which Issui drew his water. One night, a man passing by stopped at the hermit's cell and asked for shelter for the night. Issui provided this, but also saw it as an opportunity to attempt to convert the traveller to Christianity. The traveller turned out to be vehemently opposed to this, murdering the hermit and robbing him of the few possessions that he had.

Issui was canonised, and the murder spot became a site of pilgrimage. Over time, money left from these pilgrimages permitted the first church to be built on the site. This was a plain stone building, which was then replaced by the church that stands there today. Legend says that one pilgrim in the middle of the eleventh century left a sack of gold to pay for the original church. We know that it was in 1060 that the church was founded, so this is the right time, but it is more likely to be an accumulation of funds that allowed the construction to take place.

In the thirteenth century, an *Eglwys y Bedd*, or "chapel of the grave," was built over the burial place of Issui. The church also houses a medieval doom painting of the Last Judgement, with a memento mori in the form of a skeleton holding an hourglass and scythe, as well as a spade, reminding congregants that they will all end up in the same place as Issui in the end.

As a result of the fate of St Issui, his well—which is known in Welsh as *Ffynnon Issui*—took on the healing properties that it is said to have today. A tin cup is now provided to allow people to more easily draw water from the well, and anecdotal evidence suggests that it still does its job. One lady, visiting in 2009 following major foot surgery the year before, was helped by friends down the steps to the well. After bathing her foot in the water, she returned back up the steps a short while later more easily than she had gone down. Meeting her consultant at their next appointment, he could see that the foot had healed perfectly. Prior to this, the surgery had left her with ongoing pain.

Another place of pilgrimage founded by a hermit is the Chapel of St Govan. This one is a little harder to access, being built into the side of a limestone cliff overlooking the Atlantic Sea near Bosherston, also in Wales. The chapel was built in the thirteenth century and is reached via a set of well-worn stone steps from above. The religious importance of this site probably predates the building itself by some centuries.

There are a couple of different stories surrounding Govan himself. One suggests that he was an Irish monk living at

Wexford who travelled to Wales later in life, where he went to find the family of the abbot who had originally educated him. However, he has also been connected with tales from the Mabinogion, particularly with Pwyll and the Arthurian character of Sir Gawain.

Legend tells that Govan, who died in 586, was chased by pirates who had either come from Ireland or were operating out of the island of Lundy off the North Devon coast. He was able to conceal himself where the chapel now stands because a fissure opened up in the rock, closing behind him and allowing him to emerge to safety once the threat had passed. Govan founded a place of worship in response to this miraculous event.

There was, as with St Issui, a holy well on this site, which was also said to have healing powers. The water here has now dried up, but the belief in the power to heal still remains, having now been ascribed to the red clay soil on which the chapel is built. Wishes are, however, still made at the well in the hope that they will be granted.

Accessible from the simple chapel interior is the cave which formed St Govan's original hermit cell. Grooves in the stone here are said to be an imprint of the ribs of the saint, made as he was passing through, and his handprints are also said to be visible on the floor of the cell.

A curious story has arisen surrounding a silver bell belonging to St Govan, which it was said he kept in the tower of the chapel. Pirates (again) heard the bell being rung and were drawn by its sound, climbing the cliff and stealing the object. The bell was returned to the site by angels who came down from above to intervene. To protect it from future threat, they encased the bell inside a rock on the shoreline which became known as the Bell Rock. We cannot say how this story arose, but it certainly does not take account of the fact that there are some six hundred years between Govan's death and the chapel with the tower being built. This would have made it rather tricky for the saint to put his bell there himself.

Pilgrimages don't only take place to sacred sites; they are also often in connection with churches which are the homes of what are termed "holy relics." These relics, as well as being venerated for their very existence, are often said to have some sort of miraculous property, and so are a sort of "legitimate" magic which might sometimes be apotropaic, sometimes of a healing nature, or sometimes something else.

A holy relic, in its most strict sense, is a part of the mortal remains of a saint or powerful religious leader, but the description can also be extended to objects which had been in their possession. We find relics particularly in the Roman Catholic Christian Church and Buddhism.

Veneration of the relic as a form of honour is the primary reason for visiting one, but sometimes, there may be a secondary gain that can be sought. This is the case in the earliest Christian mention of such an item. In the book of the Acts of the Apostles, it is written that handkerchiefs which had touched St Paul whilst he was in Corinth where he was preaching, took on the ability to heal the sick and could also be used to drive out demons.

The most important aspect of a relic is what it represents and how it is viewed by the Church and those who come to see it. One of the biggest topics of debate around any relic is, generally, its authenticity—and this is pretty much always impossible to verify with any certainty. The problem was exacerbated at the time of the Crusades when a plethora of alleged relics found their way into Europe from Asia and the Orient. It has long been joked that Jesus must have been circumcised hundreds of times for the number of foreskins that he has had in various churches over the years.

The fate of one of these has proved to be a lasting mystery, since it disappeared in 1983. The foreskin relic in question had been kept in Rome at the Church of the Holy Name, so-called in remembrance of Jesus's own circumcision and naming day. It had been presented in AD 799 to the then-pope, Leo III, as a gift by King Charlemagne. Each year, on the Feast of the Holy

Circumcision on the first of January, a procession would pass through the village of Calcata where the relic was carried by the priest and could be seen and venerated by everyone.

However, as the nineteenth century moved into the twentieth, churches were beginning to be viewed as old-fashioned, and the ongoing problem of dwindling congregation numbers were already starting to show. The Vatican began to put a stop to anything that might show its ceremonial side as being culturally outdated, and part of this was to stop relics such as the foreskin from being discussed in written articles and the like.

Despite this, the procession was allowed to carry on—at least until the disappearance of the relic, which has never been found. A number of theories have been proposed for what happened to it. Some think that it was sent back to the Vatican, others that it was stolen and sold, and, of course, some people just blame Satanists.

The holy foreskin is not the only magical relic which has multiple contenders for the actual article. We know of at least three spears which are believed to be the lance which belonged to the soldier named Longinus, who was said to have pierced Christ's side while he was on the cross. This was the last of what became known as the Five Holy Wounds of the Passion which, as we saw in the previous chapter, are thought by some to be represented by the five points on the pentacles that we sometimes find incised in the stonework of churches.

The Holy Lance has been said to have had supernatural, magical properties for a long time. In fact, even at the time that he pierced the body, we might see this as being the case. The Bible describes how, when the body was pierced instead of the legs being broken— because Christ was already dead at this point—blood and water flowed from its side. This liquid, according to Christian legend, cured Longinus of an eye condition which he suffered with. The implication in this story, one presumes, is that even after Jesus has died, his power is such that he is still capable of healing the sick.

This miraculous healing is probably a later addition. It is certainly the case that the view of holy relics having magical powers became more common in the Middle Ages, and it is maybe at this time or a little before, that the idea spread that whoever had the lance in their possession also had the destiny of the world. This would certainly explain why various places vehemently claim authenticity of their lance, despite the fact that the Vatican itself does not vouch for any of them. The three most well-known Holy Lances are housed in St Peter's Basilica in Rome, the Hofburg Palace in Vienna, and at Vagharshapat in Armenia.

The bones of saints who died as martyrs, whether whole skeletons, skulls, or fingers, are commonly found in churches and are equally difficult to authenticate. In some cases, material analysis could be used to pin down their age, if nothing else, but the Church authorities will often not allow these sorts of tests to take place, deeming them to be sacrilegious.

As international travel became easier, large numbers of people in the nineteenth century began leaving their own countries and travelling to America; with them travelled a lot of their traditional practices, including the display of the remains of saints and the like.

The Church of the Most Holy Redeemer is on E. 3rd Street in the East Village of Manhattan and it is home to more than 150 relics of various saints, housed in a reliquary shrine in a chapel adjacent to the altar. Amongst these is the first complete skeleton, said to be the bones of a saint which was sent to an American church.

The bones are said to belong to St Datian, a saint about whom virtually nothing is known in terms of their life's work. The skeleton is encased in a wax effigy, which lies beneath the altar in the shrine. The remains of the saint came into the church's possession quite late. Up until 1892, the relic was in the possession of a wealthy Italian woman who kept the skeleton in her private chapel. When she became too poor to be able to continue living in the manner that she was and afraid that the skeleton would be seized from her by the Italian government, she donated the bones to the church.

Five years later, in 1897, a curious connection was made between the relic and a policeman who was attempting to foil a robbery at the church. At some point around this time (suspiciously, all of the reports seem very lacking in detail), someone was said to have broken into the church and stolen a prayer box. A police officer gave chase, but in the process, was fatally shot. A story then seems to have persisted until some point in the 1940s that the bones belonged to the police officer—impossible, of course, since the relic had already been in place for five years before the robbery supposedly took place.

It seems likely that the bones in the Church of the Most Holy Redeemer are those of what have been termed Roman "catacomb saints."

On 31 May 1578, workers from a nearby vineyard discovered a hollow running along the Via Salaria, a road in Rome along the southern tip of the country. Exploring inside, they found that the hollow led to a catacomb which was full of bones. These were probably the remains of many of those who were persecuted in the years following the emergence of Christianity for converting to the faith. It's estimated that over half a million people were killed at this time, with their bodies being put into the extensive Roman catacomb system.

During the Reformation, when anti-Catholic sentiments were running high, many churches were vandalised and robbed, and large numbers of Roman Catholic relics were destroyed. When they found out about the discovery of the catacomb bones not long after it had happened, the church authorities realised that here lay a solution to their problem.

They decided that the law of averages should decree that, as there were so many hundreds of people's remains in the Via Salaria cache, a number of them had to be early Christian martyrs. They would be able to send some of these bones to the affected churches, where they would replace the ones that were lost or stolen. As with the fact that we cannot establish the authenticity of most relics in any case, it did not matter if they weren't the actual bones—they would represent the same thing, and this symbolism would help to restore the faith of the congregations whose churches had been ransacked.

But which bones should be used? The Vatican employed a couple of techniques which we might think are of a slightly dubious—or, at best, ambiguous—nature. Firstly, they would look for any bones whose resting place was inscribed with a letter "M." This, they decided, stood for martyr. A vial which had once contained liquid had obviously been the repository for saintly blood. Finally, people professing psychic ability were sent into the catacomb by the church in order to pick up on the aura of martyrdom that any of the bones were giving out.

Many of these bones were wrapped in fine cloth and set with jewels. Some were encased in wax in the same manner as the bones at the Church of the Holy Redeemer which are interpreted as the vague St Datian.

By the nineteenth century, many of the remains of these catacomb saints were being dismissed across Europe, as more enlightened people began to question where they had come from and the methods which had been used to identify them. Maybe this is the real reason that the nameless Italian woman who previously had the relic of St Datian chose to give it away rather than any other. We will probably never know.

Wax has also been used to aid with the preservation of human remains which have shown remarkable, maybe magical, preservation abilities.

The Basilica di San Crisgono is a fourth-century church dedicated to St Chrysognus, another martyr, and was one of the first parish churches to be built in Rome. In a small chapel found within the main building is a glass coffin which contains the remains of Anna Maria Taigi.

Anna was born into a poor, working class family in Siena, Italy on 29 May 1769, and moved to Rome at the age of six when her father's business failed. After a basic education, she worked to help to support her family until she met Domenica Taigi, who she married in 1790 when she was twenty years of age. Her husband was, in the words of the decree that later bestowed her sainthood upon her, "rough and uncultured and his temperament undesirable." In other words, he had a bad temper.

Despite his manner, the couple were in love and had seven children, although they lost three in childbirth. Anna learned to be patient and forgiving, and her calm nature often also quelled her husband's temper.

Anna turned to the Church and was notable as being very devoted to the faith, charitable, and of a good nature, even finally managing to persuade Domenica of the luxuries of life. In 1802, she joined the Secular Trinitarians, a religious community who bear the name of the Trinity. She was bestowed various holy gifts, the most significant of which was a series of visions in which she was able to see past and future events in a solar globe.

These visions appeared slightly above Anna's head, looking like a fiery sun with a circle of thorns, and two further thorns surrounding it.

Anna died in 1837 during a cholera epidemic, which, according to some, God had told her would not affect Rome until after she passed away. Pilgrims soon began to visit the site of her grave. In 1868, it was discovered that her corpse was an incorruptible, the clothes that she was buried in having rotted away, but the body still being perfectly preserved. In 1920, when the body was again checked, it was noticed that the face and hands had started to show signs of decay, and so they were covered in wax versions, the face covering having been moulded from her death mask.

In the Catholic Church, incorruptible bodies are believed to signify the holiness of the person who appears to be avoiding full or partial decomposition. It is no longer classed as a miracle by the Church, but those who believe see it as a supernatural happening.

Arguably the most famous of the various incorruptible bodies is that of Bernadette Soubirous, known as Bernadette of Lourdes after the place where she had her visions of the Virgin Mary.

Possibly one of the oldest of the incorruptible burials for whom there is supposed to be a remaining part today is that of Etheldreda, a Saxon Princess born in 630. When she died as a result of the plague in 679, Etheldreda was buried in Ely Cathedral in a plain grave. A few years later, it was decided that her body should be moved to a larger grave that was more appropriate for her status as a princess. At this time, it was found that her body was incorruptible. People took this as a sign that she was a saint and capable of miraculous things, and she was often called upon for magical healing of throat problems.

Today, the church dedicated to St Etheldreda sits in Ely Place in London. Previously Anglican, it was purchased by the Catholic Church in 1874. In light of her healing attribution, an annual ceremony called the Blessing of the Throats still takes place in the church.

Beside the altar in St Etheldreda's Church sits a jewelled box made of wood, which is said to contain the saint's hand, still not decayed, despite being more than 1,350 years since the plague killed her.

It seems to be clear that magic can exist in the church and the churchyard in many forms, and this magic may apply equally to the Christian worshipper and the practitioner of older faiths. Saints have been able to divine the future through fiery visions just as parishioners from the village have tried circling the church and waiting in the porch to divine the same.

Sometimes, these two things can cross quite closely.

One day, a new vicar was assigned to the church at Derwent Woodlands in Derbyshire. A short while after becoming incumbent there, the vicar discovered that he was expected to follow an old tradition and preach the Sermon of the Dead. This custom involved the vicar going to the church on the last Sunday of December and, at midnight, preaching a sermon to the empty church. The church would soon not be empty, as the spirits of all those still living who were going to die in the next year would appear in the church to hear the sermon.

The vicar did not believe in such superstitious nonsense. It was the work of witches and heathens in his mind, and so, he refused to follow the tradition. And he continued to refuse to follow it—until, just before midnight on the last Sunday of December, the vicar found himself in the church, about to preach the Sermon of the Dead.

Which he did. And as he preached, the spirits of all those who were going to die in the next year took their seats in the pews, downstairs in the main church and upstairs in the gallery. There, among the figures sitting listening, the vicar saw a spirit in his own image.

Within a year, the vicar passed away.

The church at Derwent is no more either, in 1944, the whole village was submerged beneath the waters of the new Ladybower Reservoir. The spire of the church, emerging from the surface of the water, was left in place as a memorial to the village that used to be, until 1947, when it was deemed to be unsafe and was blown up.

A sad end to a church where a previous vicar had a sad end.

CHAPTER SIX

MEETING THE DEVIL AT CHURCH

In the last chapter, we saw a myriad of examples of magical practices based in and around the church. You may recall how running around a church seven times on a moonlit night and then performing some ritual with the keyhole would bring forth the Devil.

Upon first tackling this subject, it feels like a bit of a no-brainer. If the church is considered to be a house of God, then, of course, the Devil is likely to be hanging around somewhere on the periphery. He's not going to let all that worship and goodness go unchecked, surely?

But remember, this is a folklore book. And folklore is rarely so clear-cut. If you pause for just a moment and think about it, your first consideration should be to think about what we actually mean when we talk about "the Devil."

There isn't the space here to have a major theological or philosophical examination of this character, but suffice to say that the Devil is somewhat complex. He may appear under many names and in many forms, for a start. The Devil should be seen as a logical concept in terms of the development of a religion. If God is goodness and light, how can he allow people to suffer or tolerate evil? This thorny issue is addressed through a concept called theodicy. The earliest text that we know of which attempts an explanation for this is the Book of Job, which is believed to have been written around 600 BC. God tests Job through the mediation of an angel named ha-Satan.

The name *ha-Satan* means "the obstacle," and his role, much as that ascribed to the serpent in the Garden of Eden, is to place barriers in front of humans which force them to make a decision between a good and evil outcome.

It is from the Hebrew angel ha-Satan that the more common Satan develops, not immediately, but over time and by degrees until we end up with the fallen angel and enemy of God that we recognise today. The broader English term of Devil, coming from the Greek root *diabolos* represents the same thing.

A key time period in terms of our understanding of the figure of the Devil as we see him in folklore today is the Middle Ages, or the medieval period, which covers the time between around AD 500 and 1500. Certainly, during this period, the church made good use of the Devil in order to teach its moral messages: be careful not to stray from a righteous path to ensure that your soul is fit for Heaven, avoid the temptations that the Devil may throw in your way, do not be enticed towards offers or wealth or prosperity that may bring your ruin—much safer to give your money to the Church or the monarch to be sure!

Whilst the Bible is vaguer than one may realise about the concept of Hell, this, of course, became a threat of eternal damnation and punishment which could be held over the heads of the congregants. Equally vague in terms of detail in the Bible itself is a description of the look of the Devil. The way that we see both of these things possibly became culturally embedded around the start of the fourteenth century with the publication of Italian philosopher and writer Dante's poem "The Divine Comedy."

Although the image of the Devil that we picture today does not have the three faces of Dante's version, the grotesque figure with wings that he described did not have to develop too far to become the horned persona with cloven hooves and long tail that is something of a stereotype now. Whilst there had been earlier depictions in art along similar lines, such as in the 1308 icon *Descent to Hell* by Italian painter Duccio, the image would continue to be consolidated in medieval Church art. We should remember that, at that time, when fewer common folk were well educated and most certainly could not read, art was used by the Church as a method of instruction. For that reason, depictions of demons, Hell, and the Devil were common in churches and befitting of the "fire and brimstone" sermons which were commonly delivered then.

These days, we find the Devil at church frequently in terms of folklore, but not so much in terms of physical representations. He, or members of his entourage, might appear in decoratively carved roof bosses, grotesques, and sometimes an occasional piece of stained glass, but not much outside of this. There are a couple of historical reasons for Satan's cancellation in the church in this way. The first comes from changes in doctrine and thinking following the Reformation. The second, and most destructive, might be traced to the Victorian Restoration period, where much of the colourful and interesting decoration inside our churches was plastered or whitewashed over.

Even today, some of this lost art is still being rediscovered. In 2012, at St Clement Church in Outwell on the border between Norfolk and Cambridgeshire, a set of twelve medieval grotesques were rediscovered in the church roof. The carvings were heavily blackened and were spotted by accident by historian Dr. Claire Daunton through a pair of binoculars that she was using to observe difficult-to-access stained glass.

These figures proved to be of particular interest because, from the ground, it appeared as if the demons were bearing over the nearby images of the apostles. However, when examining the carvings up close, it became apparent that they were actually hunched, perhaps beaten down by the word of God, with the apostles standing over them. Church art depicting the victory of good over evil is generally very clear, and so, the ambiguous nature of these carvings when viewed from the church floor makes them very unusual.

The Devil might be conspicuous by his absence at church in terms of artistic rendering, but he is certainly fairly easy to spot in terms of folklore. Whilst the Catholic view might suggest that the Devil would stay away from a church building through fear, tradition (along with superstition, which we will explore in the next chapter) certainly has no qualms about placing him there.

When we look at the architecture of a church from a folkloric perspective, there is a much-repeated idea that suggests that the door that may sometimes be found in the northern wall of older churches is known as a "Devil's Door." Stories say that the door was placed there to allow the Devil egress from the church. It was thought in the Middle Ages that the Devil would be a part of a child's soul until baptism, at which point an exorcism would essentially take place to remove the evil presence. Folklore suggests that the Devil would then flee through the door.

From a more historical standpoint, there is little to substantiate this idea, however. There are links between the north side of the church and the Devil, which, again, stem from the Middle Ages. One theory suggests that church buildings were frequently built on the north side of a pathway in order to allow for an entrance to come from the south side. Additionally, we have already discussed the fact that many Christian churches stand on sites which had earlier places of worship on them. During the transitory period when both Christian worshippers and the unconverted shared the space, the north door would allow access to the latter—the Devil's side of the building being deemed more appropriate for their use.

We do need to balance this theory against the more practical idea that churches were built closest to where the largest collection of houses in a settlement was located. Churches would have had doors in both the north and south walls, and, in some cases, the northern door was the more significant of the two.

It is quite likely that the folklore surrounding these doors mostly rises from the Victorian period, when interest in the magical, the occult, or the otherworldly was bordering on obsessive in some cases. Recollections of medieval beliefs naturally helped to fuel a narrative surrounding the role of the Devil, meaning that it was not a giant leap to surmise that the number of these doors that were bricked up by this period was due to a desire to prevent the Devil from being able to get back into the church he had once been driven out.

Furthermore, this probable nineteenth-century linking of the fleeing Devil with the church door demonstrates a lack of understanding of the rite of baptism. It is true that the Devil was linked with unbaptised children in the medieval period, but the Sarum rite of baptism, which was made formal in the eleventh century, was a two-part process. The first part, which included salt being placed in the child's mouth and both the priest and the acolytes signing the cross on the baby, at which point the priest effectively exorcises it, took place in the church porch. If the church had no porch, then this part of the rite took place at the door. In other words, the child had already been exorcised before it was brought into the church.

In actuality, of course, the doors had been sealed for a much more practical reason. Prior to the publication of the Book of Common Prayer in 1549, processions were a common part of a church service, re-enacting events such as Christ's entry into Jerusalem. The congregants would process through the north door, for example, around the outside of the church and back in through the south side. When the changes instigated by the Church of England stopped such practices, the north door became superfluous in many churches. Bricking up the door would both prevent draughts, helping to keep the church warmer, and would also provide more space for the installation of box pews when these came into fashion.

Maybe some kind of remnant of these processions is present in a curious apparition which took place in the Church of St

Peter Ad Vincula, meaning "St Peter in Chains," in the North Devon village of Combe Martin. The witness, an artist, was staying with friends in the village in the late summer of 1921. She had attended an evensong service which was followed by an organ recital, and her vision took place after these.

The lady was surprised to see a door in the church's rood screen open and a procession emerge, led by an ecclesiastical minister who she believed was a bishop, due to his mitre and crozier. He was dressed in a long, cream-coloured gown, adorned with gold and buttoned down the front. Following him were a number of other priests in similarly coloured robes, and, after them, six men carrying a tray measuring around four feet square. On top of the tray was a model of a walled-and-gated city, which appeared to be constructed of fawn-coloured wax.

Following behind this unusual structure were then lined up a number of courtiers in more brightly coloured coats and ladies wearing pointed Heninns, the conical headdress and veil worn by European noblewomen in the late Middle Ages. Bringing up the rear were numerous people in peasant garb.

A friend of the witness, to whom she evidently relayed the story, noted that the lady in question had studied costume as part of her work as an artist, and could, therefore, vouch for her accuracy when she described the clothes as belonging to the fourteenth century.

However, her knowledge of period dress doesn't appear to have stretched to Church practices. When I spoke to historian and folklorist Dr. Francis Young, who is also a lay Reader for the Church of England, about this vision, he pointed out that the most senior ecclesiastical figure would always bring up the rear of such processions. The laity and the clergy would also not mix in this way, and the former would not even be allowed past the divide of the rood screen.

The artist was in the church with other members of her family, but they saw nothing unusual, so this vision appears to have been personal to the witness.

Staying in the North Devon area for a moment provides a useful bridge to the subject of the Devil as a central figure in cautionary tales. The swarthy, handsome, and mysterious man wooing young ladies to what could be their potentially terrible fate until it transpires that he is the Devil in disguise is a common folkloric motif which has been much-repeated in modern literature and filmed entertainment.

One story relates how a young girl named Molly decides to go to Barnstaple Fair in order to try and find a potential partner. However, little does she realise that the Devil is also fond of the fair and so, of course, they end up meeting each other, with him in his disguise as a strangely desirable man. He begins to visit her house as part of their courtship but, like some kind of reverse-vampire, he always leaves before the lamps are lit for the evening. Perhaps his glamour is transparent by candle flame?

Eventually, the girl finds herself in a predicament of the Devil's making. Investigating a cacophony of noise from Molly's room, her father and some servants discover her wedged between the bed and the wall by some strange force. Nobody is able to approach her to give any help. Eventually, after everything else has failed, the Rector of Ashford is called in. He is known to have skills working with the forces of evil and, indeed, he is able to outwit the Devil in this case.

The Rector lights a candle and makes a bargain with the Devil that Molly will become his, but only if he waits until the candle is fully burned out. Once the Devil has agreed to the terms, the clergyman blows out the candle, places it in a box, and bricks the hole up in the wall of Marwood Church, where it is supposed to still be found to this day. A very similar story is found elsewhere in North Devon where the Devil tells a girl that he is courting that she may have the time it takes a candle to burn out to get changed for their date. At that point, on the previously sought advice of a local vicar, the girl's mother blows out the candle and runs to the vicar, who hurriedly seals it into the wall of his church.

There are numerous other examples. The stories, in most cases, are probably a hangover from the Victorian and Edwardian morality tales which abound in folklore, but they possibly have much older roots in the idea of encasing a candle in a building. When we think back to the idea of the foundation sacrifice and the earlier examples of human sacrifice for similar purposes, we note that, when such practices were stopped, they were replaced with walling up something else to symbolise life. Sometimes this might be an egg, and sometimes a candle was used.

The Devil does not only pose a threat to women in the laity, of course, and can be equally problematic for women in religious orders. In these cases, he rarely tries to date the women but is rather looking to turn them from God to follow him instead. Such was the case with Isabelli Tomasi, an ancestor of the notable Italian author Giuseppe Tomasi di Lampedusa. Entering into orders in a Benedictine convent when she was just fifteen, Isabelli took the name of Sister Maria Crocifissa della Concezione, or Sister Maria Crocifissa of the Conception.

On 11 August 1676, when Sister Maria was thirty-one years of age, she was discovered on the floor of her Sicilian convent cell in some distress. The nun's face was covered in ink, and she was clutching a handwritten note made up of a strange mix of letters and other symbols. Nobody was able to make sense of the missive, which ran for fourteen lines.

Sister Maria declared that the letter had been written by the Devil, who seemed to have possessed the woman in order to do so. She said that he had appeared and tried to persuade her to turn her back on God and her holy orders.

The letter remained a mystery for centuries until recently, in 2017, code-breaking decryption software was employed by Italian scientists to try and get to the bottom of the mystery. They started with the premise that Maria would probably have known ancient languages and vocabulary, and it turned out that the letter did contain elements of Runic, Greek, Latin, and other words, as well as other shorthand and symbols.

The scientists managed to decipher far more of the text than they were expecting. Their results suggested that, in part, the text read:

> *Humans are responsible for the creation of God. This system works for no one. God thinks he can free mortals. Perhaps now, Styx is certain. God and Jesus are dead weights.*

Modern thinking naturally suggests that Sister Maria was either bipolar or was suffering from a form of schizophrenia. It was not uncommon to hear her screaming at night, according to historical records, and she was prone to fainting at the altar. She frequently warned her peers that the Devil was trying to cause them trouble. A contemporary account written by Abbess Maria Serafica suggests that the Church believed that Sister Maria was struggling with a number of "evil spirits" rather than the Devil himself.

Evil spirits can take many forms, and the Devil is said to employ many minions in his work, ranging from malicious demons to more mischievous creatures. There are a number of examples of "imps" to be found in church carvings to represent the latter of these. They are often tricky to spot, which puts them in line with many other representations of the mischievous sprites in art as well as in architecture. They are often hidden away in images, revealing themselves only to the particularly observant. There might be a couple of reasons for this.

Firstly, imps are generally described as being particularly small beings, so they would not necessarily be foregrounded. Secondly, and perhaps of more relevance, we find many examples of imps being contained in objects in order to serve a particular purpose, such as in boxes, bottles, and even weapons. Author of the *Discworld* series Terry Pratchett famously used this idea when describing the "iconograph" —a magical object which functioned like a real-world camera. An imp was given brushes and pencils and placed in a box with a hatch on the front. When the hatch was opened, the imp would draw what it saw really quickly. The idea was built upon in the novel *Moving Pictures,* with a multi-imp variation which worked like a movie camera.

Much like the grotesques at St Clement Church at the beginning of this chapter, a small, demonic carving was alleged to have been discovered in Chester cathedral as recently as 2015. A film crew working with archaeologists as part of a project called "Chester Unlocked" were granted special permission to use a drone camera inside the cathedral, which grew out of the church of a Benedictine abbey established in 1093. Upon watching back footage captured by their drone, the archaeology team spotted a carving of a small demon, bound in chains, close to a window in the nave.

Stories suggest that a medieval priest who was overseeing the construction of the nave saw the Devil staring through one of the windows, and so, commissioned a stonemason to carve the image of the demon in chains in an attempt to scare the Devil off.

However, not everything here is as it seems. Not only was the Chester imp known about for many years prior to the drone capture, but it had been talked about in guidebooks for the cathedral and Chester history for a long time. This makes perfect sense, because, if the suggestion put forward by the Chester Business Improvement District development group that historians were only then labelling the carving (in 2015) the "Chester Imp" were true, how could the legend already exist without the carving being known about?

Furthermore, the drone footage did not reveal the carving for the first time, because it is clearly visible from the floor of the nave, albeit somewhat small to the naked eye. Additionally, the imp was often found as a design feature on historic objects in the area: on door knockers in the eighteenth century and on teaspoons and toasting forks in the Victorian period.

In an amusing postscript, it would appear that the editor of *The Daily Mirror* newspaper had at least bothered to fact check the story when it was picked up by a reporter for the newspaper, although the efforts were in vain, as the article ended up being published despite being marked as unsuitable. Even at the time of writing for this book, the online edition of the newspaper for 25 June 2015 still carries the reporter's name in the byline as "Steve White-do-not-use"!

More well known, and probably slightly less controversial, is the carving of an imp in Lincoln Cathedral, which legend says was actually a living imp that was petrified and remains on the building.

The story here relates how the Devil, annoyed with the construction of Lincoln Cathedral, sent two imps to the building to cause disruption. They were responsible for smashing windows, breaking lights, and generally being annoying, so, an angel was sent down to put a stop to their cavorting. One imp was scared of the angel and concealed itself underneath a table. The second was more bold and taunted the angel, throwing stones at it and defying the messenger from God to stop it.

The angel, losing patience, did indeed stop the imp by turning it to stone, where it can still be seen at the top of a pillar overlooking the Angel Choir—the choir stalls in the cathedral named for the number of representations of angels found there.

At least, that is one version of the story. Over the years, there have been many additions and variations to this basic outline. The second imp ran off afterwards, where it might have remained outside the building, waiting for its companion to return. This version is used to explain the windy conditions in the area. There are certainly folk tales connected with the Devil using the cathedral to escape the wind there which may be connected.

Alternatively, the second imp ran off to Grimsby, where it began to cause similar problems at the minster until, once more, an angel came to sort it out. This time, the angel smacked the imp on its rear before turning it to stone. This version explains a carving in Grimsby Minster of a figure who appears to be clutching at his rear whilst supporting the stone column on his shoulders. In this case, the carving is very well worn and does not look like an imp. More likely, it is a human figure bearing the stone.

The story of the imps at Lincoln Cathedral has also been conflated with the folklore surrounding the twisted spire of St Mary and All Saints' Church at Chesterfield which, as we learned in the first chapter, has a whole range of stories attached to its curious shape. It has also been claimed that the imps were responsible for this too.

Whilst the Angel Choir was constructed during the period from 1250 to 1280, suggesting that the carving and some of the associated stories have an early origin, the association with imps began much later. It is not clear exactly when the term "Lincoln imp" began to be used, but it most likely at some point between 1869, when antiquarian and folklorist Richard John King mentioned the carving in his *Handbook to the Cathedrals of England*, and 1897, when G.T. Hemsley published a pamphlet under the name Arnold Frost.

Being especially interested in folklore, it is highly likely that King would have referred to the imp using that name if it was in common use when he wrote his book. Instead, he describes the grotesque as looking like "an elf with large ears," suggesting that it might be illustrative of the folklore of the period in which the Angel Choir was constructed.

By 1897, the term "imp" must have come into use, because Frost uses it extensively in his pamphlet, *The Ballad of the Wind, the Devil and Lincoln Minster: A Lincolnshire Legend.* The publication, in fact, would be both enlarged in a second edition in the same year and then "improved" (the publisher's own term) the following year, as more information about the legend came to light. As well as describing the "cult of the Lincoln Imp" as being something that "Oxford men" were trying to appropriate, Frost also refers to the carving as such as part of his poem about the legend:

The bishop we know died long ago,
The wind still waits, nor will he go
Till he has a chance of beating his foe;

But the devil hopp'd up without a limp,
And at once took shape as the 'Lincoln Imp.'
And there he sits a'top of the column,
And grins at the people who gaze so solemn;
Moreover, he mocks at the wind below,
And says, 'you may wait till doomsday, O!'

In the introduction to the pamphlet, Frost claims that the information was based on an old legend from Lincolnshire that had not been in print previously, but which he had heard from a sixty-year-old North Lincolnshire man who had been told it by his own father when he was a boy.

There was a previously known expression whose meaning was to look at someone or something with envy. This phrase "look as the devil over Lincoln" can be traced back in literature to at least the middle of the sixteenth century and probably explains the idea of the Devil wanting to claim Lincoln Minster for his own.

Lincoln Cathedral now sells the imp in keyring form. It is a common souvenir in the area, mostly as a supposed bringer of good luck, and has been since the early twentieth century when a local jeweller named James Ward Usher managed to secure the sole rights to reproduce the image for profitable gain. The legend, as we have seen, includes no indication of the imp being a bringer of good fortune, but this is now probably the most prominent folklore associated with the creature.

The idea of the second imp causing the high winds to blow around the outside of the cathedral while it waits for its companion may feel a little like a bolt-on to this story, but it is, in fact, a much more widespread idea. Looking across Europe, we find a number of examples which connect windy conditions around churches and cathedrals with the Devil himself. Often, this also include the idea of waiting.

In the French city of Autun, a Burgundian legend tells how the Devil arrived at the cathedral, bringing the wind with him. Upon arrival, he discovered that the canons and clergy were arguing a point arising from the church's reunification but had not been able to reach agreement. Saying that he would be able to settle the argument and bring peace in a short space of time, the Devil entered the cathedral building. However, even his powers were not enough to stop an ecclesiastic disagreement, and so he is still there whilst the canons continue their dispute. The wind blows endlessly around the building while waiting for the discussion to be resolved.

The story, of course, makes little religious sense. Why would the Devil seek to help the clergy and bring peace? It's not one of his core skills, after all. The narrative is more likely to be a commentary on either the reunification process by those who disagreed with it, or on the nature of the clergy in Autun themselves.

A very similar tale to that of the Lincoln imp is situated at Strasbourg Cathedral. Versions from the mid-nineteenth and early twentieth centuries tell how the Devil, bored from sitting around in Hell, summoned a wind from the German highlands. Travelling on this wind, he alighted in Strasbourg, where he entered the cathedral while the wind continued to whip around the square outside. Seeing the Devil for who he was, a preacher caused him to become stuck to one of the church pillars. The wind still waits outside, blowing in its impatience.

This seems to be a variation of another story in which the Devil arrives at the cathedral and spots a representation of himself in the pediment—the triangular-shaped stone which sits on top of the portico and is common in classical architecture. Being somewhat vain, the Devil thinks that, if he is on the outside of the building in this fashion, then the interior must be even more wonderful. However, once inside, he is bound by a charm and is unable to leave again, with the wind once again remaining in wait.

Undoubtedly, the Devil would have been pleased with the design of some of the stained glass at Strasbourg. A number of the cathedral windows depict demons terrorising humans. We see them in Hell, burning those who have strayed from the path of righteousness, and also on Earth, where they attempt to corrupt saints to turn from God, and worse.

As we have previously learned, using church art to reinforce the dangers of living a non-Christian life was not uncommon in the Middle Ages. Far more unusual is finding the Devil being used on a church building as a form of protection against attack by other supernatural forces. This was the role more usually given to the protective Black Dog known as the Church Grim, which we examined in detail in Chapter Two, or through the use of a variety of apotropaic marks, as previously discussed. A potential example of the Devil taking on this mantle can be found in Southern Sweden.

The parish of Raus in Helsingborg is home to Raus Kyrka, a medieval church built in 1150, which is now the oldest preserved building of the period in the area. During the fifteenth century, a number of modifications were made to the building, including a number of ceiling paintings of biblical images, which were then lost during the Reformation when, like in so many other churches, they were whitewashed over. It was also in the fourteen hundreds that a stone head was set into the wall above the main entrance.

We cannot say for certain who or what the head depicts. One suggestion is that it shows a local giant who was responsible for the construction of the church. In Sweden, it is a common motif for giants to be instrumental in the building of churches. Another says that it may be a medieval Christian knight. The most common modern belief is that it is an image of the Devil which was placed there to protect the church from trolls.

In this latter case, the legend that backs this tells how a local troll interfered with the construction of the church because of his hatred of the sound of the church bells. He tried moving the stone to the other side of the stream each night, but this failed when the builders simply moved everything to the location on which the church now stands and built there instead. This caused the troll to move to nearby Kullaberg.

The main problem with this story comes from the fact that we now know that the stone head was a later addition to the building, and logic would dictate that three hundred years is perhaps a little long to wait after being troubled by a troll before you add protection against any of its kin. This aside, it is an interesting and unusual example of the idea of the Devil protecting a church building against other folkloric creatures, whether or not the head is actually showing the Devil or something else.

The parallels are obvious here between the story of Raus Kyrka and those that we explored in the first chapter involving fairies. As well as the numerous examples of the fairies attempting to disrupt church construction, it is also very well known that they have an aversion to church bells. Like many of us, they probably just like a lie-in on a Sunday morning without interruption. In the Devon town of Ottery St Mary, the inspiration for Ottery St Catchpole in the *Harry Potter* universe, the attempts by the fairies to silence the church bells are still celebrated to this day. On the closest Saturday to Midsummer's Day each year, local school children dress as pixies and fairies and enact a ritual "capturing" of the town's bellringers.

The Devil too, it turns out, is not a fan of the bells, and there are various stories relating to his attempts to steal them from church towers. The Grade II listed St David's Church at Llanarth, situated in the Welsh authority of Ceredigion, has a belfry containing three bells dating back to 1776. The Devil's expedition to steal one of these was thwarted when he made too much noise and woke the local vicar, who sent him packing. As he jumped from the building to the churchyard beneath, he landed on a stone which forever bore his footprint afterwards.

A similar, although more detailed, story is found at St Mary's Church in Newington, Kent. The tower here contains five bells, which the Devil once tried to steal because of the amount of noise that they made. He succeeded in climbing the church tower and stuffing all the bells into a giant sack, but the weight of this was so great that, when he jumped to the churchyard below, he once again left an imprint in a stone there.

The curious thing about the thirty-eight-centimetre-long footprint on the Devil's Stone at St Mary's, aside from the fact that it is raised like a welt rather than forming an impression, is that it does not look like a cloven hoof, but rather resembles the sole of a giant brogue. Evidently, the Devil was looking particularly dapper that day. The stone now stands next to a metal sign noting that it was moved from the corner of Church Lane to its current position in 1938.

There is more to the story here. The Devil lost his footing on jumping down from the church tower and the bells fell from the sack, rolling into the Libbet Stream, which flows nearby. The villagers made numerous attempts to retrieve their bells, but each time they failed, and the bells fell back into the water.

After some time, a witch who was passing through the area saw their predicament and offered them a solution. She said that the bells would only be able to be raised if they were hitched to a pair of white oxen (or in some versions of the story, four of the same).

The residents of Newington took the woman's advice, and everything appeared to be working well, until a small boy shouted out (in the annoying way that small children do) that one of the oxen had a black spot behind its ear, or on the end of its nose. Typically, versions of the story don't seem to be able to settle on this detail. In either case, as soon as the proclamation is made, the bells fall back into the stream and they are never seen again, although local folklore tells us that bubbles are still found in the water at the very spot at which they were lost.

Nothing here is unique in terms of its folklore. There are numerous examples of church bells being lost in the sea or in other stretches of water. Often, they are heard to ring out in ghostly fashion on stormy nights. Lord William Bottreaux ordered bells for the Cornish harbour village of Boscastle which were lost at sea, and which legend tells us can still be heard ringing from both Boscastle and Tintagel when the conditions are right.

Even the story of the oxen, which seems to be a very specific detail, is found in other places associated with different stories. For example, close to the Devon village of Bow stands the site of the former Nymet Tracy Castle. In the early twentieth century, the remains of the walls here used to stand three or four feet above ground level. It was not uncommon for stone from sites such as this to be repurposed for building at that time, and so, a man from the village went with the farmer on whose land the remains were located to help to draw some of the stones to mend the farm lane.

This task proved to be more difficult than they imagined, and even harnessing horses to the stone was fruitless. The two men stood pondering what they should do when they heard a voice call out from somewhere, "you will never move this stone until you get an old man with a white beard and two white oxen." Whether they managed to locate such assistance remains unrecorded.

An additional, and probably later, belief associated with the Devil's Stone at St Mary's is that, if you place your finger on the top of the stone and walk round in a prescribed number of times—usually three—then this will ensure that you have good luck. Nothing found within the original story would indicate why this should be the case, which hints that the idea developed later based on other similar folklore from elsewhere. We already saw at the very start of this chapter how walking round the church itself could be employed to raise the Devil.

Another St Mary's Church, this time in Bungay, Suffolk, sees a similar superstition attached with a stone in the churchyard, rather than the church itself. A glacial erratic here has some very confused folklore attached to it.

The first confusion surrounds the name of this stone, which is commonly given as the Druid's Stone, but which is also referred to as the Devil Stone or the Giant's Grave. The term Devil Stone refers to a belief which we will return to in a moment when we unpick the rest of the confusion. Much of the folklore that we see in the landscape relating to the Devil, in terms of the names of places and features has, as noted by folklorist Jeremy Harte in his book *Cloven Country*, grown out of earlier examples of stories which feature giants as the protagonist. The dual names here would seem to back that view up.

The more common name, Druid's Stone, is typical of so many features in the landscape which claim without any evidence to have Druidic origins, often just because they are old and unusual. This problematic viewpoint was championed by many antiquarian clergymen scholars, but originally popularised by William Stukeley. Indeed, the Druid's Stone was incorrectly described by a local antiquarian and recorder or ley-lines in 1926 as a fallen monolith.

Moving on to the superstition side, popular folklore records that the Devil may be summoned by circling or knocking on the stone twelve times, thus giving the granite slab its alternative name of the Devil Stone. This is actually a conflation of two separate pieces of folklore. It was said that children would dance around the stone seven times on a certain day of the year in order to see the Devil. The reference to twelve rotations or knocks comes from a different superstition which young girls would act out. After undertaking this part, they would then place their ears against the stone, believing that they would hear the answers to whatever questions they wished to have answered.

Bungay is more well known in terms of its folklore by being one of the two churches which was said to have been visited by a demonic black dog during a great storm on 4 August 1577. The animal caused havoc in the church and left its claw marks burned into the door, as we learned in Chapter Four.

Stories such as the visit by the demonic black dog rise up as an old superstitious explanation for natural events which are not fully understood. In the case of the storm of 1577, it is probable that the churches were directly struck by lightning, and even possible that rare ball lightning formed and rolled through the building.

A similar set of freak weather conditions probably hit the Church of St Pancras in the picturesque Dartmoor village of Widecombe in the Moor on 21 October 1638. This time, the Devil was held responsible for the damage after lightning struck the church with such ferocity that one of the pinnacles of the tower exploded and plummeted to the churchyard below.

In this case, the legend that developed was one that served the purpose of describing what might befall anyone who didn't keep the Sabbath holy or didn't pay proper attention in church. The Devil, it was said, came to the church on that Sunday in order to claim the soul of one of the congregants, Jan Reynolds, who frequently paid no attention to the sermon and was playing cards at the back of the church. On arriving at the church, the Devil tethered his horse to the pinnacle and, as he rode off, pulled the pinnacle down. The story tells that, as they galloped off, the four aces fell from the pack of cards that Jan was carrying. There are four medieval field enclosures nearby which are known as the "Four Aces." With a bit of imagination, you can see the rough shapes of playing card suits in their perimeters.

Whilst these sorts of stories were needed in the past to provide the explanations for the things that science or medicine could not, in later years, thinking became more enlightened and understanding improved. So, when the parish church of Morchard Bishop in Devon was struck by a meteorite in January 1952 and lost a pinnacle in a similar way, the church simply put the meteorite on display for everyone to see.

Sometimes, the bells aren't enough for the Devil, and he attempts to steal even more than that. This was said to be the case at St Mary's Church in Marston Moretaine, Bedfordshire. This has a very rare example of a detached church tower, with its particularly thick walls at the base of the structure suggesting that it was probably a watchtower of refuge at one time in its history. Legend says that the tower was, at one time, attached to the church as normal, but that the Devil had tried to steal it. However, he found the structure too heavy to carry and dropped it just a few yards from the main building, where it can now be seen.

The Church of St Bueno in the Somerset village of Culbone is probably the smallest parish church in England, measuring just thirty-five feet in length and with a capacity of thirty seats. The main building is certainly old, having been recorded in the Domesday Book, but has been altered a number of times, including the addition of a porch in the thirteenth century and nave in the fifteenth. A small spire was added to the church in 1888. This looks strangely out of place when compared to the rest of the building, and maybe it is this fact that led to a strange recent legend explaining how it got there.

Situated some three miles away in the town of Porlock is the thirteenth-century Church of St Dubricius. In 1703, a storm here damaged the spire of the church, which today has a flat top. The much more entertaining folklore, however, says that the Devil broke wind spectacularly when passing through Porlock, blowing the top of the spire through the air, where it landed in its current position atop St Bueno's. The tiny spire of the Culbone church certainly looks like it would fit very comfortably on top of the Porlock one.

There has been a suggestion of another story involving the Devil moving a spire situated in Kent and seemingly connected with tales involving St Dunstan. This reference tells that he picked up the steeple of the church from the village of Brookland, being chased across the border into Kent by St Dunstan, who finally caught up with him, grabbing the Devil by the nose with a pair of tongs and causing him to drop the steeple close to Hastings.

There seems to be very few mentions of this story to be found and no obvious credible sources for its origin. What seems to be the case here is that a local variation has formed around the more well-known story of St Dunstan and the Devil, which has given rise to a range of folkloric variations over time.

The core story tells how the tenth-century St Dunstan, who became Archbishop of Canterbury after having lived a more reclusive early life, met the Devil in the grounds of Glastonbury Abbey. Dunstan passed his time as a hermit by making metal tools for the monks of the abbey. An old man came to Dunstan one day with a request for work, the nature of which varies depending on the particular story, but the saint recognised him as the Devil. Not showing his recognition, Dunstan put his tongs into the fire, leaving them there until they were red hot, at which point he removed them and used them to grab the Devil by the nose. Depending on the version of the story, he does not let the Devil go until he has admitted that he will not cause any more trouble, or until the Devil agrees that he will not enter any house which is protected by a horseshoe hanging over the door.

For its part, the story of St Dunstan is, again, just a reworking of an older one, given a Christianised retelling in order to embed the ideas of good winning out over evil. The original story, commonly referred to as "The Blacksmith and the Devil," is the oldest folk tale to have been retold across Europe, having been traced back as far as the Bronze Age.

In West Yorkshire, we find a tradition with a back story that seems to bear at least some similarities to the story of Jan Reynolds at Widecombe in the Moor. This takes place at the Church of Dewsbury Minster in Kirklees, a thirteenth-century place of worship which was rebuilt in the Gothic Revivalist style in 1895.

Every Christmas Eve at around ten in the evening, the church bellringers convene to ring The Devil's Knell, tolling the church's tenor bell once for every year since the birth of Christ. The ringing is carefully timed to finish on the stroke of midnight. The custom of ringing The Devil's Knell is said to stem from a penitential undertaking by Sir Thomas de Soothill, after whom the bell, known as "Black Tom," is named.

In 1492, Sir Thomas is said to have flown into a rage after having discovered that a young boy who worked as his servant had not attended church. He threw the boy into the local mill pond, where he drowned. Seeing the error of his ways, Sir Thomas paid for the installation of the bell, which is now named after him, and began the custom of ringing the years since Christ's birth as being symbolic of the defeat of evil.

Although some have suggested that the name "Devil's Knell" comes from the ringing of the bell scaring the Devil away, it is in fact taken from the idea that the Devil died when Christ was born (although, if he did, the rest of this chapter is probably a complete lie). This is the reason why the custom is also sometimes known as The Old Lad's Passing Bell.

The Church of St Mary the Virgin in the English village of Frensham is home to an artefact that, at first sight, seems somewhat out of place in a place of religious worship. A nineteen-inch-deep beaten copper cauldron here looks as if it would be more at home in a witch's kitchen than a house of God; indeed, one of the origin stories which explains how it got there is connected to a famous local practitioner.

Mother Ludlam was a well-known "white witch" who was said to have lived in a cave in a sandstone cliff at nearby Moor Park, overlooking the River Wey and not far from the church. One day, it was said that the Devil came to the cave to try and borrow the cauldron from Mother Ludlam, who often loaned items to local people who completed a certain ritual at the cave in order to make their request. Being a clever witch, Mother Ludlam recognised the Devil for who he was, and would not allow the loan. However, the Devil stole the cauldron and fled the cave with the witch in pursuit. In a fashion common in many of our folkloric stories to explain the names of landmarks in our geographic landscape, the Devil took giant strides across the Surrey countryside, creating the hills which are now known as "the Devil's Jumps" as he did so, but he inadvertently dropped the cauldron on Kettlebury Hill. Mother Ludlam was able to retrieve her cauldron and then place it in the church to stop the Devil from being able to take it back, where it remains to this day.

There are a surprising number of other stories related to how the cauldron came to be in place in the church. One has a similar theme, but tells that it was fairies in the area, rather than the witch, who would loan items. A man who borrowed the cauldron from the fairies failed to return it to them, and so, the fairies placed a curse on the man so that the cauldron would forever follow him round. In despair, he took sanctuary in the church, where he died and where the cauldron remained afterwards.

Another version says that it was a man who borrowed the cauldron, but from Mother Ludlam. Again, he failed to return the item, and the witch became very angry, so the man hid the receptacle in the church in fear.

Whichever story you like involving the Devil, the fairies, or the witch, they are all far more exciting than the probably true nature of the cauldron, which was most likely used to brew ale for the community at large church gatherings. It appears to have been a part of the fabric of the church as far back as anyone can trace.

The Devil never seems to have learned the valuable lesson that he should put on a pair of shoes in order to evade capture. St Dunstan recognised him by his cloven feet, and Mother Ludlam likely did the same. The landlady of a public house at Poundsgate on Dartmoor told, in reference to the story of the Devil visiting Widecombe Church to claim the soul of Jan Reynolds, that he stopped there for a drink, apparently in the guise of a man. She, too, clocked his feet.

But are these all just old folk tales consigned to our superstitious past, right? Maybe not—at least not according to the details of an event told about St Michael's Church in the Old Town neighbourhood of Chicago in the 1970s.

The Devil's visit supposedly took place during evening mass. Being a Catholic church, the congregants were lined up to receive Holy Communion from the priest. One of those attending seemed rather out of place compared to the others that evening, being dressed in a dark robe which had a hood that prevented the wearer's face from being seen. As the figure approached the priest more closely, the holy man said that he heard a deep-sounding snort come from beneath the hood.

Looking down, as in the older stories, the priest saw not a pair of shoes, but rather black, pointed hooves.

The Devil, if it was he, did not, as you would expect, accept the communion wafer from the priest, but disappeared, leaving the next celebrant in line to continue with the ceremony.

The story of the Devil at St Michael's has been retold many times since the 1970s, but, frustratingly, in each case, the details are virtually identical, and the name of the priest concerned has never been included, so we have to be slightly wary of where the original version might have come from. However, it is worth noting that a number of other people since have reported seeing a cloaked figure in the church during mass. Do these apparitions get reported in memory of the original story, or is there more at play here?

After a significant reconstruction, the Church of St Michael's only stood for a short time following its dedication in 1869 before the Great Chicago Fire ravaged the city for two days, reducing St Michael's to a shell. Maybe the gusts of wind, known by the locals as "fire devils," caused a suggestion that the Devil was somehow involved in the church's destruction. Or perhaps there is a link, thanks to the iconography of the main altar in the church which depicts St Michael himself, with his sword and shield, casting Satan down from Heaven, as commanded by God.

As we have already seen, it is often the Devil's minions in the form of demons that are depicted in churches, rather than the man himself. Usually, these are not identifiable, but are rather more generic in their design, instead just being used to remind those in the congregation what's likely to happen if they don't behave themselves.

One fun exception to this is a demon known as Tutivillus, who can be found surviving in a number of carvings, such as in the roof at Ely Cathedral, or on a fifteenth-century misericord at St Laurence's Church in the English town of Ludlow. Tutivillus is associated with writing and literacy, and, aside from carvings, he would often appear in medieval church wall paintings. Some of these still survive today without having been obliterated during the Reformation, such as a faint example in the church at Little Melton in Norfolk.

As the demon linked with the written and spoken word, Tutivillus has a couple of different connections. One is with those who use language professionally, such as printers or publishers. In old manuscript illustrations, he can be seen peering over monks as the scribe, willing them to make errors.

However, his connection to the church once again has more to do with the congregation behaving correctly during a service. Tutivillus would eavesdrop on the conversations of those in the pews and would make a note of their gossip or idle words on a parchment or scroll that he carried with him for this purpose. One of the stories found about him in old sermons describes how those attending mass talked so much rather than paying attention to what was being preached that the demon had to stretch his parchment out with his teeth in order to be able to record everything that was said. Often, this causes the parchment to break, which causes such a commotion that the priest explains to the congregation what has happened and they duly repent, meaning that Tutivillus has to go back and erase everything that he wrote, much to his chagrin and the priest's pleasure—an obvious morality tale.

Developments in the character of Tutivillus led to him also having a role collecting words during Latin services which were not pronounced correctly or were muttered under the breath. This connects with the idea of him trying to get scribes or typesetters to make mistakes. All of these misspoken words would be stuffed into a bag or sack and taken to Hell, where they would be kept so that, at the time of your judgement, you would have to account for them.

Tutivillus's name forms the etymological root of the word *tutiviller*, which emerges first in the sixteenth century, describing someone who gossips or otherwise damages a person's reputation through their words.

So, if you found any errors in this particular chapter, then please remember that they are not mine, nor are they the fault of my publisher. Tutivillus did it.

CHAPTER SEVEN

SUPERSTITION IN CHURCH AND CHURCHYARD

A FRIEND OF A FRIEND (yes, we all known the implications of that phrase through urban legends, but this one is verifiably true) fell pregnant after following a superstition connected with a church.

When Kateryna Pokotylo was newly married, she went on holiday to Turkey with her husband. On one of the guided sightseeing tours that they took, they visited Demre, which is built on the ancient city of Myra, said to be the birthplace of St Nicholas. The tour took in the old church in the town dedicated to the saint and, whilst exploring the architecture of the place, the guide drew people's attention to a hole in the form of a star on the eleventh-century mosaic floor. Here, according to local tradition, any prayers which were made fervently would be heard and answered by God.

Being newly married and with thoughts of children on the horizon, Kateryna prayed at the spot for a baby girl. She fell pregnant that same year...and had a girl.

When we examine folklore through the lens of our ancestors, superstition plays a massive role in the day-to-day lives of ordinary people. Folk magic, healing, family life, and work all brought ritual and superstition into play. In the same way that charms would often use a mix of magical work and biblical verse, farmers might employ ritual custom and folk belief, alongside prayer or church attendance, to bless their crops and their work. Divine intervention is good…but why put all your eggs in one basket?

Superstition is, perhaps, a difficult concept to pin down exactly. What it means very much depends on your approach to it. The *Merriam-Webster Dictionary* defines superstition as:

> 1. *a: a belief or practice resulting from ignorance, fear of the unknown, trust in magic or chance, or a false conception of causation*
>   *b: an irrational abject attitude of mind toward the supernatural, nature, or God resulting from superstition*
> 2. *a notion maintained despite evidence to the contrary*

What this definition shows, probably above anything else, is that anyone's belief system relies on their own personal faith. Anything that falls outside of that might be deemed to be based on "superstition." Of course, personal belief systems also have their own superstitions too.

The word "ignorance" is a difficult one to negotiate. Whilst it can refer to something about which people have no experience or cultural understanding on the one hand, it is also a loaded term when it comes to folklore. This is because the predominantly white, male, urban folklore collectors of the nineteenth century, whose work so many now reference, employed the term in a derogatory manner when talking of the rural or working classes.

Not everything in the world can be satisfactorily explained from a scientific viewpoint. This doesn't mean they are magical or otherworldly, but it also doesn't mean that they aren't, at least from a folklore perspective. These are things to be borne in mind as we explore some of the superstitions connected to the church and the churchyard.

We will start in the churchyard and work our way in towards the church interior.

Superstition will often come into being around structures or objects that are particularly unusual or dominate others around them. In the first chapter, we learned about the tomb of Richard Cabel and the common idea of circling the grave a number of times in order for something specific to happen. In my book *Dark Folklore,* I have written about the grave of Mercy Brown in the Baptist Church Cemetery in Exeter, Rhode Island, which is unassuming in itself, but notable because of a family vampire myth connected with it. People leave offerings at this site or follow other rituals in order to try and raise Mercy's spirit.

The largest cemetery in Paris is the Cemetery of Père-Lachaise. It opened in 1804 and now covers 110 acres. It is the world's most visited necropolis, with over 3.5 million people a year walking between the tombs, probably because of the number of well-known people who have been buried there.

Amongst these, although not as well-known as some of the others such as Jim Morrison or Oscar Wilde, is a journalist, Victor Noir, who wrote for the French newspaper *La Marseillaise.* When the editor of the newspaper was challenged to a dual by Prince Pierre Bonaparte, the famous Emperor's cousin, Noir was sent to arrange the details of the meeting. Whilst doing so, when tempers became frayed, the prince shot him. The murder led to Victor Noir becoming a revolutionary symbol in the country.

Although originally buried in his hometown, Victor Noir's body was moved to Père-Lachaise in 1891 as an act of commemoration. The famous French artist Jules Dalou was commissioned to design and make a bronze sculpture for the grave. The memorial he created was a life-size depiction of Victor, lying down in his clothes as if the murder had just taken place, with his top hat at his feet.

The figure is rendered in great detail, with every hair and coat button looking as if a cast had been taken of the man himself. However, a particular set of superstitions has arisen around this grave because of one particular detail which Dalou included.

The artist decided, for whatever reason, to endow the figure of Victor Noir with a more than adequate bulge, which did nothing if not demonstrate that the man dressed to the left. As the years passed, this feature led to the development of rituals which used the grave to symbolise fertility.

Much like Kateryna's prayers at the start of this chapter, Victor Noir's grave can be used for a more folkloric intervention in the desire to get pregnant. Rubbing the bulge and dropping a flower into the top hat is said to increase fertility in women. Additionally, to secure pregnancy (rather than just a good time), they should rub his right shoe, or the left for twins. If you are not quite that far along your journey, then kissing the mouth of the figure will bring you a quality lover.

A further tradition has formed from this where those who successfully became pregnant after following the superstition come back to the grave later and place offerings, along with photographs of their children, in and around the hat.

Being more than a century old, the bronze on this statue has long since oxidized, giving it the greenish hue which we see on so many statues on plinths in our towns and cities. Apart, that is, from the well-rubbed areas. The nose and mouth of the face, the famous trouser area, and the ends of both feet are well-polished, as to retain their original bronze colour.

A similar effect has happened to the statue of the famous Skye Terrier Greyfriars Bobby which stands on a granite plinth opposite Greyfriars Kirkyard. Bobby was the faithful pet of John Gray, who had joined the Edinburgh police as a night watchman in 1850 after failing to find employment as a gardener. After he died of tuberculosis in 1858, Bobby spent the next ten years at his master's graveside. He defied all attempts to remove him and, eventually, a shelter was erected for him at the grave. Local residents would look after Bobby; he left the grave at one each afternoon and went to John Gray's favourite coffee house, where he was given a meal.

The statue was unveiled in 1873 and, since that time, people have been touching the nose of the dog for good luck, again leading to that section being free of oxidization.

At one time, the French authorities attempted to prevent women from touching the statue of Victor Noir any further, putting up a fence to stop access, as well as a sign declaring that indecent rubbing or graffiti would lead to prosecution. This caused such a public outcry that the fence was torn down and the grave remains open.

Intervention to try and prevent superstitious ritual in other churchyards has had similar effects in the past.

The parish church of St Martin de la Bellouse on the island of Guernsey, one of the Channel Islands, dates from 1225, having been built on the site of a previous place of worship from the eleventh century. This land has a Neolithic tomb which might be connected to a stone menhir known as *La Gran'mère du Chimquière* (Grandmother of the Cemetery).

The menhir dates back to a period somewhere between 2,500 and 1,800 years before the birth of Christ. The imagery is certainly Pagan and may be goddess-related in some way (although that is debatable), but has also been reworked later, as the face is more distinctly Roman.

The tradition of leaving tokens of coins, or flowers, at the menhir has persisted for a long time. At some point, a warden of the church attempted to stop this and had the statue broken in half, but everyone was so annoyed by this act that they rescued the pieces and had them cemented back together, so that the *Gran'mère* still stands now. Brides who are married at the church will place flowers on the head of the statue to invite good luck.

There are many superstitions associated with graves aside from these more notable examples. Some have made a grave better known. Some are more general. In either case, as with much of folklore, we have to be very careful to unpick the claims, to separate the old beliefs, that seem to be the case from misunderstandings that change the narrative.

We have already seen how the mortsafes that were used to protect graves from resurrection men have been claimed as devices to keep vampires and other undead from rising from the earth. Some sources also attribute the mortsafe at the Old Parish Burial Ground over the grave of Seath Mor in the Scottish Highlands that we discussed earlier in the book as being put there to protect people from the curse.

Misunderstandings also surround a tomb in the churchyard of St Clement's Church in the Essex town of Leigh-on-Sea. The church is dedicated to the first-century martyr, Clement, who is also the patron saint of mariners (which is not surprising considering its elevated position looking out over the harbour).

Standing outside the entrance to the church is an altar tomb which contains the remains of Mary Ellis, who died in 1609 at the age—according to her inscription—of 119. Whilst this is not impossible (with the oldest woman to have lived whose age could be independently verified being Jeanne Calment of France, who died in 1997 at the age of 122), it seems highly unlikely for someone who was living in Tudor times. The vagaries of Tudor mathematics have been offered as a possible explanation, but even this seems a stretch.

It is not Mary Ellis's advanced age, however, which has made this grave notable. That comes from the deep score marks which can be found in the lid of the tomb. These have led to its becoming known as "the Cutlass Stone."

Legend here suggests that the stone was used by members of press gangs to sharpen their swords. Between the seventeenth and nineteenth centuries, the Royal Navy needed a seemingly endless supply of men to go to sea and fight its battles. Groups of unsavoury men would form themselves into gangs and wait in the area of buildings, such as churches or public houses, to find men who were fit and able. These men would be captured and forced into conscripting for service, with the gang members being paid an amount for each person they provided.

Drinking establishments would often have places for people to hide to avoid being captured by the press gangs, such as tables with false lids which could house a body inside, or the equivalent of priest holes.

The story at St Clements is that, by sharpening their swords on the stone, the press gangs made enough noise to alert the congregation that they were outside, giving time for the young men to flee the church via a tunnel which ran from under the tower. Only women, children, and the elderly would remain, and were of no use to the gang.

It is a nice story, which has many flaws, aside from the obvious one that even the press gang ruffians would not be stupid enough to keep making the same mistake and provide an early warning system day in and day out. There is no evidence of any such tunnel running underneath the church. It is inevitably the case in terms of folklore that, when a story mentions a secret tunnel or passage, there will not be one. In this case, the idea may come from a suggestion that a tunnel used by smugglers ran from the nearby rectory to the old town. There is little evidence for this either.

Buildings archaeologist Dr. James Wright, author of *Historic Building Mythbusting*, has disputed the origins of score marks such as those on the Cutlass Stone, particularly with reference to the alleged "arrow sharpening mark" which are frequently found in castles and other historic fortified buildings. He confirmed my suspicions in the case of this tomb lid as well.

The central crack on the lid looks to be too significant to have been caused by blade sharpening and seems more akin to a fault or fissure which has opened up over time. The smaller marks certainly do look like they would have been made with a blade, but James pointed out that this was unlikely, not only because the position of some of them would be very difficult to get either a sword or other blade into, but also for the more significant reason that running a blade across this sort of stone would actually have the opposite effect to that intended and would dull the blade rather than sharpening it. This was the reason that people carried portable whetstones for sharpening.

A more mundane explanation than the press gangs has also been offered for the Cutlass Stone marks, namely, that they were produced by workers sharpening their scythes before cutting the grass in the churchyard. Again, using the stone would have the same effect of dulling the edge as it would have with a sword, and it is unlikely that the Church authorities would have not found out that the practice was happening over a period of time and put a stop to it.

James's research and experience leads him to conclude, with regards to the score marks that are attributed to medieval archers, that ritual folk medicine has a large part to play, with the marks being made through repeated people harvesting holy dust to use as a powder to be added to either water or communion wine as a curative, or for some other benefit. Records of this from the medieval period can be traced forwards many centuries later.

For example, in the case of Mary Ellis's grave, it is quite possible that this could be the case because people were trying to obtain the same kind of long life that the inscription said that Mary enjoyed (even though she most likely didn't). In this scenario, they would have scraped dust from the easiest place, where there was already a score mark, thus deepening them over time. By mixing a tincture using this dust, they would have hoped that it would have improved their life expectancy.

There are many superstitions associated with graves. Much like the score marks on the Cutlass Stone, some of these seem to arise from misunderstandings, misinterpretation, and repetition of information which is accepted as being accurate when it isn't. At the same time, there are others that are more legitimately traceable. We need to try and separate one from another as best we can.

One of the problematic superstitions cited by some is that headstones on graves used to be sited over the feet in order to stop bodies from rising from the grave, and that they have only later become memorials at the head of the grave. This belief appears to conflate a number of different ideas, some of which are fairly clear and others which are more speculative.

Many of the ideas surrounding weighting corpses come from fear of revenants rising to terrorise the living from Anglo-Saxon times. These, however, centre for the most part on deviant burials—the interment of social outcasts. There is also archaeological evidence to suggest that, in some medieval burials, the dead may have been mutilated in an effort to prevent them from rising again. (However, this might relate to times of pandemic or in areas of plague or other illnesses as a response to concerns about the spread of disease.)

Placing slabs on or at graves may also have a confused origin from the Jewish tradition of piling rocks onto graves, sometimes forming small cairns. This took place for a number of reasons. Since prehistoric times, people have stacked stones on graves to mark the site as a burial and to try and stop animals from digging up the remains, and these have gone on to form memorials. Jewish families held a belief that, if a priest came too close to the deceased, he would make them impure, and so the rocks were a preventative measure.

More recently, placing stones onto graves can be symbolic of keeping the deceased in place in reference to the Talmud stating that the soul dwells in the burial place. Sometimes, the placing of a stone is as simple as marking that a person visited the grave and prayed there.

Taphophobia is the fear of being buried alive, and there have been many famous sufferers. George Washington requested that his body was laid out for three days before being put into the ground. Hans Christian Andersen asked for his arteries to be cut open before burial, whereas the Polish composer Chopin went one stage further and requested the removal of his heart. Superstitions relating to the prevention of premature burial coupled with urban legends about corpses with long hair or exhumed coffins with fingernail marks on the inside of the lid, led to the development in the eighteenth and nineteenth centuries of a number of different safety coffins.

One of these was a system designed in 1829 by Dr. Johann Gottfried Taberger, which used a series of strings to allow a bell to be rung above ground, which would alert workers in the churchyard. They would, then, be able to introduce air into the coffin until it could be dug up. The idea built upon an earlier impractical suggestion from German priest P.G. Pessler at the end of the eighteenth century that coffins should be fitted with tubes which would allow cords to be connected to the bells in the church belfry.

Some believe that this is the origin of the phrase "saved by the bell," but that is purely folk etymology. The phrase did not begin appearing regularly in print until the early twentieth century, gradually becoming more figurative after its initial literal uses, which came from the world of boxing. Possibly the earliest is from *The Fitchburg Daily Sentinel* newspaper in 1893, which noted that "Martin Flaherty defeated Bobby Burns in 32*[sic]* rounds by a complete knockout. Half a dozen times Flaherty was saved by the bell in the earlier rounds."

Suggestions that the safety coffins also provided the origin of the phrase "dead ringer" make even less sense. The meaning of the phrase is totally unconnected with graves, coming as it does from the nineteenth-century term for a duplicate (ringer) and precise. It was used in horse racing slang in this period.

There was a superstitious practice, which continued into the nineteenth century, of placing coins on the eyes of a deceased body before it was buried. In Ancient Greek and Roman times, this stemmed from the mythological story of the need to pay the ferryman Charon in the underworld in order to buy safe passage across the River Styx. Without such payment, the soul would not be able to find rest. From this mythological root, placing coins on the eyes in terms of Christian burial can be viewed as a mark of respect, but it also stems from a superstitious belief that, if they eyes are not closed, then the dead will look for another person to take to the grave with them.

Some research suggests that the payment to Charon as a story became a more Christianised sacrament. After a miracle declared by Pope Innocent III in 1213 in which some coins had been changed into communion wafers, we see some possible evidence that both coins and wafers had been placed in the mouths of corpses through superstitious beliefs that this would afford supernatural protection. This was clamped down on heavily by Church authorities in the case of the communion wafer, but the use of coins seems to have been less common and so was, for the most part, ignored.

Interesting variations on these practices were recorded in Devon in 1904 with relation to the village of Morchard Bishop and were published in *Devon Notes and Queries,* and then, subsequently, in the twenty first report of the Folklore Committee for the Devonshire Association. These funeral customs noted that coins were placed at the feet of the deceased, one on each foot, and that different values were used depending on the age of the person who had died.

Children up to three months old had a farthing (one-quarter penny) placed on each foot, children up to six months a half-penny, and a penny up to the age of one year. After this, silver coins should then be used, but without any particular amount being stated.

Whilst all of the other coins could be left as they were, the farthings had to have a hole drilled through them. This was to "let the devil out," and there may be some connection here with the fact that children who had died so young may well have done so before they could be baptised.

Folklore relating to the souls of unbaptised children being unable to move on and find rest can be found all over the world. For example, in Sweden, these souls are called *Mylings,* and they are confined to the Earth until they can find another person to bury them. The Myling will jump onto the back of someone out walking during the night and ask to be carried to the nearest churchyard. The closer to the church they get, the heavier they become, until it becomes a struggle to move. If the person bearing the Myling does not reach the churchyard, then the Myling will kill them and begin looking for another carrier.

We see similarities here with the Scandinavian strandvaskare that we examined earlier, and some tie-ins with the motifs of both cockstride ghosts and sleep paralysis, although the victim is awake and walking in this instance.

It was also recorded from the Morchard Bishop area that three particular items should be placed into coffins before they were buried: a piece of silver, a fragment of cloth from whatever the person was wearing when they died, and an herb from their garden. If the deceased's garden did not contain an herb, then someone was required to walk a distance of at least three miles to acquire one from a different garden.

The piece of silver might, again, possibly be seen as a form of payment, maybe to St Peter, to get through the gates of Heaven without difficulty, and the cloth might serve as some sort of indicator as to the identity of the soul. The meaning of the herb is more difficult to ascertain, because there is no record of which particular one should be used, if indeed it should be a particular one. The walk of three miles is also puzzling in terms of its meaning.

However, it is not necessary to walk quite as far as three miles for a grave superstition. Superstition considered it bad luck to walk across a grave, both in America and in Britain, and this belief links to the common expression that "someone has just walked over my grave" when we get a sudden feeling of unease or an unexplained shiver through our body.

In the England of the Middle Ages, there was a firm belief that the place that you would be buried when you died was predestined. At this time, therefore, the concept from which the phrase derives centred around the idea not that someone had walked over a physical grave, but rather that they had passed over the piece of ground where you would later be buried.

The expression was not in use at this time, however. That came later. We see it used very clear with reference to the predetermined burial spot in a nineteenth-century novel called *Basil Godfrey's Caprice*: "Joan shuddered – that irrepressible convulsive shudder which old wives say is caused by a footstep walking over the place of our grave that shall be."

The earliest use of the phrase in print appears to be from the famous author Jonathan Swift, writing under the name of Simon Wagstaff, in 1738 in a book entitled *A Complete Collection of Genteel and Ingenious Conversation*.

In some American variations of the expression, animals are sometimes mentioned instead of people, particularly that "a goose walked over my grave." It is not clear how this variation came about, but, possibly, the word "goose" was added later from the idea that being cold or shuddering unexpectedly is also accompanied by the raising of the skin in what we colloquially call "goose bumps."

The strongly held superstition now is simply that it is bad luck to walk on a grave. This also applied historically to graves that were left open overnight, because to do so would soon invite another death to the community. As this belief probably arose as a deterrent to stop people from straying near dangerous open holes in case they fell in, then that at least could have easily come true.

A churchyard superstition which has less-clear origins in that you should hold your breath when passing by one. This seems to still be done by a number of people. One high school student from South Carolina, for example, interviewed as part of folklore fieldwork, stated that they did so because it would be disrespectful otherwise to those in the graves who were no longer able to breathe. To disrespect the dead might be to invite a haunting.

Others believed that, if you did not hold your breath, then you might "inhale" and take on the spirit of one of the deceased.

Having the spirits of the dead latch onto you can happen in other ways in some cultures, too, as we have seen earlier in a couple of different ways. Sometimes, it was thought that pointing at a grave would cause this. In other superstitions, pointing at a grave would cause your finger to fall off. We are all taught that it is rude to point, and these are some more extreme examples.

Prior to burial, a funeral service will normally have taken place, and a number of superstitions exist around these. In the Christian Church, there are various days on which funerals cannot be conducted, most particularly Holy Thursday through to Easter Sunday, out of respect for the time of remembrance of Christ's crucifixion, but also on Sundays during Advent and Lent.

In the first chapter, we briefly noted the tolling of the "death knell" with a single bell as part of funerary traditions. At one time, three different bells would be rung when it needed to be declared that someone was dying. The first of these, the passing bell, would warn that a death was likely. As we have seen, the death knell was then used immediately after death.

The last of the three bells, and the one which is used in modern funerals, is the corpse bell. Now, this is a single tolling bell, rung slowly with long gaps between each sound, but traditional ringing was more communicative. The death knell used a chiming technique known as a teller, using different sequences of bells to impart news about the deceased.

The bell would be tolled three times twice to make a total of six chimes if the deceased was a woman and thrice three times if they were male. This would be followed by a single toll for each year that the deceased had been alive. Through this system, those in the wider community would, hopefully, be able to work out roughly who had died. These practices had been written into Canonical Law in the sixteenth century by monarchs Henry VIII and Elizabeth I and continued until the nineteenth century.

Sometimes, professions would also be communicated using the funeral bell. The tolling for a fireman, for instance, was found its origins with the telegraph, when the word "fell" would have been communicated with a series of five dashes, followed by a pause, and then two more lots of five dashes. This was translated to the pattern of tolls.

Another bell-related superstition pertaining to fire told that, if the town clock should strike whilst the church bells were ringing, then this would predict that a fire was going to break out. A belief recorded in Somerset in 1929 said that, if the church clock struck while choir were singing during a church service, then this would be foreshadowing a death within the year.

It is said that there was a bell-ringing tradition at St Michael's Church in Coventry known as the "Pudding Bell." Used in the nineteenth century and rung shortly after the end of Matins, folklore tells us that this bell was tolled so that the people who remained at home knew that everyone would soon be leaving and should, therefore, take the Sunday meal out of the oven.

It is very unlikely that this was the case, as, traditionally, everyone was expected to attend church. It is possibly a story that refers to the suggestion that a bell used to ring if Evensong was going to take place earlier than usual, or it might have been attached to a memory of the prayer bells that used to be rung during the war. Or it is apocryphal and just an amusing tale.

In more superstitious times, church bells would be rung in an effort to frighten away evil spirits, but this practice would then be outlawed by the medieval Church authorities. Of course, this didn't mean that it might not still happen from time to time, both for this reason and for other purposes.

Around the turn of the twentieth century, a Mr. T. Cann Hughes heard of the bells of the parish church in the Devon town of Dawlish being rung during a thunderstorm. The belief was that the spirit of the bells would overcome the spirit of the lightning. Although this church, St Gregory's, is Anglican, the superstition about the bells was common in Roman Catholic countries. The Roman Catholic Bishop of New Jersey was noted to have blessed a chime of bells for this purpose in New York in the year 1855.

Dawlish is a coastal town, and this may be connected to maritime traditions to ensure plain sailing, but the ringing of bells to repel lightning was not an uncommon superstition. Some surviving church bells of a sufficient age have been found which are inscribed with the Latin words *Vivos voco. Mortuos plango. Fulgura frango.* In English, this translates roughly to "I call the living. I mourn the dead. I drive away lightning."

It was also believed in the medieval period that the houseleek would also repel lightning, so, they were sometimes grown on the roofs of churches, as well as domestic dwellings. The houseleek is not a vegetable like the edible leek, but a common name for a succulent of the *Sempervivum* family.

Nobody would want to listen to, and rely upon, church bells to tell them of someone's death if there was a chance of finding out much further in advance who might be about to die, and so we find divinatory practices centred around the church porch for this purpose. Many of these seem to have become conflated, but the most recognised time for people to do this would have been on St Mark's Eve, April 24.

The ritual for divining who was going to die in a parish in the forthcoming year is recorded as early as 1608 and continued into the nineteenth century. Being widespread across the United Kingdom, there are naturally a number of variations in the way that the ritual was undertaken, but the core element involved sitting in the church porch between the hours of eleven at night and one in the morning. Often, this would have to be done for three years in a row, and then, on the night of the third year, the spirits of those who were going to die would be seen filing their way into (or out of) the church.

In some tellings of the superstition, some of the methods of death might be visible, such as the person dripping water if they were going to drown. The ritual is recording in a poem called "The Vigil of St Mark" by James Montgomery.

'Tis now, replied the village belle,
St Mark's mysterious eve,
And all that old traditions tell
I tremblingly believe;

How, when the midnight signal tolls,
Along the churchyard green,
A mournful train of sentences souls
In winding-sheets are seen.

The ghosts of all whom death shall doom
Within the coming year,
In pale procession walk the gloom,
Amid the silence drear.

Some of the other times of the year that the vigil seems to have been conflated from also have their own unusual differences in the way they play out. The Welsh version that took place at *Nos Galan* (New Year's Eve), for example, had people spending the night in the church porch to receive the knowledge of who was to die, and, in this case, that came in the form of a voice from beneath the altar table giving the names.

At Hatherleigh, in Devon, there was a nineteenth-century variation that took place on Midsummer's Eve. Once again, men would gather in the porch of the church, and the parade of spirits of the living from the town would be seen going into the church. However, in this version, some of them would come back out again later. The people who came back out would be married in the next year. Those that did not emerge from the building would be the people who would die, and if any of the men on the vigil fell asleep while they were there, then they would join them.

The inclusion of the apparitions of people who would be married in the next twelve months reminds us of the fact that love divination was one of the most widespread forms of divination that there was. Everyone was forever trying to ascertain who their husband was going to be and trying to find supernatural ways of making sure that he was a good one; understandable at a period of history when men had so much control over womenfolk. St Mark's Eve was a good time for this divination as well.

"On St Mark's Eve, at twelve o'clock,
The fair maid will watch her smock,
To find her husband in the dark,
By praying unto good St Mark."

This was one technique, recorded in verse. The smock in question was to be hung in front of the fireplace at home to dry. At midnight, hopefully, the apparition of the man that you were going to marry would appear and turn it.

This night was also one of a few mentioned for divining a future spouse through the scattering of hemp seeds. Starting from the church porch, young women would run home, scattering hemp seeds whilst reciting some variation of a common rhyme. The ritual was first described in a book from 1685 called *Mother Bunch's Closet* which gave the verse as:

"Hemp seed I sow, hemp seed I sow,
And he that must be my true love,
Come after me and mow."

On the ninth occasion, it was expected that the apparition would be seen or a bell would be heard.

In South West England and Wales, it is notable that this divination could be carried out by both males and females seeking to discover their future partner. Otherwise, it was a ritual that was usually only undertaken by women. Men who wanted to see an apparition of their intended would normally round a church at midnight, either three or nine times, whilst carrying a drawn sword. The rhyme that they would use was: "Here's the sword, but where's the scabbard?" This seems to be somewhat disconnected with love…right up until the point that you realise that it is euphemistic.

Assuming that you have completed your divination in one piece, seen the apparition of your betrothed to be (rather than seeing a vision of a coffin, which is sometimes referred to and which was taken to mean either that you would not marry, or worse, that you would die) and then been through the appropriate courtship rituals, then, eventually, you are going to want to tie the knot. Aside from the more specific wedding superstitions, such as not seeing the bride on the night before the wedding or it being unlucky to wed in green, there are wedding superstitions which are more connected with the church as well.

For example, the timing of a wedding could have been important. It was once said that, if the church clock struck the hour whilst a wedding was taking place, then either the bride or groom would die in the following twelve months. This superstition related to the time whilst the wedding party were inside the church for the ceremony. If the clock struck the hour while the party was outside the church, then this would bring good luck, rather than something much worse.

An 1891 collection entitled *Old Church Lore* compiled by William Andrews noted that, in the eighteenth century, there were many examples of marriages taking place with the bride wearing only her shift, or sometimes a white sheet. This happened because of an old tradition which told that, if the bride was in debt and her spouse married her in this fashion, then he would not be liable to settle any of the debts that she had incurred prior to the wedding.

The arrangement appears to have applied both ways. In 1771, Nathaniel Eller married a widow named Hibbert in the

Manchester town of Ashton-under-Lyne. She wore a shift "as a means to free them both from any obligation of paying her former husband's debts," according to the report in the local newspaper there, the *Manchester Mercury*.

Probably the most colourful of any reports of such ceremonies taking place was recorded in *Aris's Birmingham Gazette* in 1797:

> *There is an opinion generally prevalent in Staffordshire that if a woman should marry a man in distressed circumstances, none of his creditors can touch her property if she should be in puris naturalibus while the ceremony is performed. In consequence of this prejudice, a woman of some property lately came with her intended husband into the vestry of the great church of Birmingham, and the moment she understood the priest was ready at the altar, she threw off a large cloak, and in the exact state of Eve in Paradise, walked deliberately to the spot, and remained in that state till the ceremony was ended. This circumstance has naturally excited much noise in the neighbourhood, and various opinions prevail respecting the conduct of the clergyman. Some vehemently condemn him as having given sanction to an act of indecency; and others think, as nothing is said relative to dress in the nuptial ceremony, that he had no power to refuse the rite. Our readers may be assured of this extraordinary event, however improbable it may appear in these times of virtue and decorum.*

A modern marriage ceremony will often conclude with the words "…and you may now kiss the bride," invariably leading to a polite kiss between the happy couple to the accompaniment of a light round of applause from the congregation.

Years ago, superstitions surrounding the chance to kiss the bride seem to have made the whole process a bit of a free-for-all. It was not common for the parents of working class or poorer couples to be at the church for the wedding ceremony. A friend of the groom would normally represent the father, and in some places, he would have the right to claim the first kiss before the groom had a chance.

In other places, the clergyman presiding over the ceremony believed that they had this right. Often it was expected and, if the vicar had recently moved to an area where this was the case, he might find the whole party just standing in place at the end of the service, waiting for the kiss to take place before they could leave. William Henderson describes, in his 1879 *Folk-Lore of the Northern Counties* a wedding where this happened and, after standing around for a long period with nothing happening, the bride just turned and kissed the vicar herself.

In Chapter Four, we made mention of St Patrick, and the folklore that suggests that he may have been responsible for the introduction of the solar cross symbol. Whilst this is perhaps more debatable, it is easier to accept the suggestion that he founded a church in the valley of Gleannindeachta, or Glynn, in the Irish county of East Antrim.

It may be that this was St John's Parish Church, the ruins of which still stand in the area. With records going back to the fourteenth century, when differences in the masonry suggest that the chancel may have been added, along with an early window. This site is one of the oldest with ecclesiastical use in this part of Ireland.

A new church was built in the western part of the old churchyard relatively recently, dated to just 1840. Designed by Belfast architect Charles Lanyon, it is a compact and tidy looking single-storey chapel.

For some reason, a local legend has formed here to suggest that the new church is home to a secret underground chamber, with a tunnel that connects it to a nearby house. The tunnel, according to the story, was used to move a large iron chest full of gold to the churchyard, where it was buried.

This is a problematic story. We know, and have already discussed, that the story of a secret tunnel in folklore usually equates to there being no tunnel at all. This tale is particularly scant on detail. Whose treasure was it? Why did they need to bury it? Who caused the tunnel to be made? With the church being less than two hundred years old, these questions should not be difficult to answer, and yet there is no context at all. Sometimes, there might be some evidence that suggests a tunnel, but its purpose would not have been what the folklore and superstition suggest.

Like the church at Glynn, the Church of All Saints in the mid-Devon town of Winkleigh also dates back to the fourteenth century, although it has been much remodelled since then. All Saints stands not too far distant from the King's Arms public house in the centre of the town. A picturesque, thatched building dating from the seventeenth century and said to be haunted by two ghosts who the locals have named Cecilia and George, a dining room now stands over the top of what was once the courtyard.

Beneath this dining room, with its top capped in strengthened glass, is a well shaft with a depth of some thirty feet. From the bottom of this well run two actual tunnels. One of these heads straight for the church, and the other away to the northwest.

It has long been said that dragons once lived at Winkleigh. One of them was said to have been driven away in 1393 by Simon De Winkleigh, whose shield bearing a red cross and gold crown hangs at the entrance to the pub building. The dragon, evidently, was not overly impressed and returned the following day to eat Simon. The shield was all that remained.

Dragons, of course, equate to treasure, and so it would be easy to make such links. Gold coins being moved to and from the church through the tunnel, clandestine trade with smugglers and the clergy taking place—these would be all the more likely if the tunnel actually reached anywhere near the church.

In 2002, a local mining group descended into the shaft and set out to explore the tunnels. They found that both of them ran for only fifteen feet or so before they terminated. It was probable that they were test *adits*—short tunnels that were dug in an effort to find good local deposits of silver—but which amounted to nothing.

Myth and superstition can continue to surround a church long after it has finished serving its purpose as a house of God. Folklore and the supernatural perhaps attaches itself more readily to these buildings simply because they have the look and feel of somewhere that mystery can pervade. Many of our abandoned churches and ruins have such stories. They act as locations for people to visit, explore, and take part in ostensive play.

The term *ostension*, in folklore, refers to the acting out of a story in the real world, or the interaction with a story in the hopes that you will experience it. For example, the tomb of Squire Richard Cabell in the churchyard of Holy Trinity Church in the Devon town of Buckfastleigh, which we examined in Chapter Two, serves this purpose when people act out the superstition of circling the tomb and putting their finger into the keyhole to see if Squire Cabell's spirit will gnaw their fingertip.

Sometimes, by acting out these legends, things that people experience may get retold and become incorporated into the ongoing legend, thus shaping and reshaping the narrative over time.

As well as being influenced by ostension, stories associated with abandoned churches are often brought into being by the influence of journalism. This is especially the case when links are made between such sites and devil worship or Satanism. Let's stick for a moment with Holy Trinity Church in Buckfastleigh as an example.

Holy Trinity, or Buckfastleigh Old Church, as it is sometimes known, sits atop a hill overlooking the town beneath. The building dated back to the thirteenth century, but on 21 July 1992 it was reduced to a shell when a fire caused some £1 million of damage.

It is generally believed that the fire was started deliberately, and this has now been firmly linked with devil worship, despite there being no actual evidence of this. The accusations have been made frequently enough in the media that they are now oft repeated as fact. Statements are used such as this very ambiguous one from the news outlet *Plymouth Live* on 15 December 2019:

> *... this beautiful 13th century parish church came to a terrible end in 1992, ostensibly at the hands of Satanists, although this was never proven.*

It was never proven because there was no evidence for it to investigate in the first place. The vicar at the time, the Reverend Paul Wilson, and his church warden stated that they "feared" that it was the work of Devil worshippers. This, however, is pure conjecture. The only comments made in relation to this were the fact that it appeared that the fire had started under the altar and the suggestion that the church had been "the venue for strange, sinister happenings" in the recent past, because some graffiti had been painted on the walls and, once, some human faeces had been smeared on the building.

None of these things really provide a tangible link to any kind of devil worship or other occult happening. Graffiti and soiling are as likely, and probably more so, to have been the result of teenagers, people out of control due to drink or drugs, or other people acting stupidly. Underneath the altar would be a logically place to start a fire if one was doing so maliciously: the altar cloth would not only hide the beginnings of the blaze but would also be suitably combustible.

Now, of course, the connection has been made and has stuck. Viewed alongside the folklore surrounding Cabell's tomb and the links with the *Hound of the Baskervilles,* it is easy to see why. Similar spurious connections have been made more than once between occultists and sheep being killed on the moors nearby.

Possibly the best-known ruined church that carries associations to occult practices and what the press likes to term "black magic" is St Mary's old church, which was classified as an ancient monument in 1961. Its listing names it as the Church of St Mary the Virgin.

The ruins of St Mary's can be found in the Bedfordshire village of Clophill. The land here is believed to have been used as a place of worship since the tenth century. The stone structure, whose remains are visible now, probably dates from the fourteenth century.

The church remained in service to the parishioners for worship until the middle of the nineteenth century, when the increasing population of the parish led to the construction of a new building in the centre of the village. Thus, in 1849, the chancel was taken down and the galleries were removed. Other alterations continued into the following year, at which point the building became a mortuary chapel. Two of the church bells had been removed, with the third being left in place to toll in the manner that was described earlier in this chapter. Bodies were still able to be buried in the old churchyard on site.

The links with devil worship were made first by the police and were then reported on in the local press. An incident took place at the church on 16 March 1963 when two boys from Luton discovered human remains in front of the stone altar in the church ruins. Police were called in to investigate and discovered that a few graves showed signs of damage and that graffiti had been painted on the walls of the church. They described this as "Satanic."

The bones appeared to have been removed from a grave belonging to Jenny Humberstone, who died and was buried there in 1770. She was the wife (although some accounts name her as the daughter) of the local apothecary for Clophill. It looked to the police as if the bones had been arranged in a particular way, and, further, the skull was impaled on a metal spike. This led to a police spokesperson commenting that "we believe this may be a case of black magic practice."

Of course, this was only a working theory, and the police did say that it "may" have been such a case. Vandalism of churches and graves has always been a problem, and there can be some quite macabre examples. In the cemetery at Greyfriars, Edinburgh (where the famous dog, Bobby, lay at his master's grave) stands the mausoleum of Sir George MacKenzie. He earned the nickname "Bloody" MacKenzie because, in his role as Lord Advocate in the seventeenth century, he had overseen the torture and ultimate death of thousands of members of a Scottish religious movement known as Covenanters. Here, in 2003, two boys, aged fifteen and seventeen, were charged with offences relating to violating graves after they broke into the mausoleum, stole Sir George MacKenzie's skull, and used it to play football.

The press naturally picked up on the suggestion of occult happenings at Clophill and, on 21 March 1963, the *Luton News* newspaper displayed their shockingly bad understanding of anything to do with the occult by running an article on the find under the headline "Voodooism Or Vandalism?" The national press then picked up the story and ran with it, and suddenly, St Mary's began to get a reputation for being "the Haunted Church."

As you might expect, this was a recipe for disaster. The newspaper coverage led to a desire for other people to visit the site in the hope that they would see something unusual. The reputation for the site being connected with occult practices naturally grew with each visit, and, through the process of ostension previously described, legend trippers led to a continued build-up of alleged strangeness ay Clophill.

The site became something of a mecca for visits after dark and troublesome behaviour. Some of this was more malicious than others. For example, on 8 May 1963, just two months after the initial gruesome find, students from Shuttleworth College were found at the site, dressed in white sheets. This was nothing more than typical student hijinks, and those responsible evidently received a dressing-down from the college principal, as the Rector received a letter of apology shortly afterwards.

A few years later, however, a group of ten youths who had travelled from the nearby towns of Harpenden and St Albans were issued with fines of £10 by the church for their behaviour at the church. Four were later acquitted, but the rest were found to be guilty. More instances of desecration were to follow.

Naturally, stories of links with Satanism and occult practices are going to rouse the interest of paranormal investigation groups—even more when the press has already named the site as "the Haunted Church." Many visits by such groups over the years have led to numbers of reports of ghosts being seen, or sensed, or filmed, in the case of a "hooded monk ghost" reported in 2016. This has led to new claims that St Mary's Church is "said to be one of the most haunted buildings in England"—you have to wonder how long the list of "most haunted" buildings in the country can become before it is not being haunted that is more notable.

Such claims, and some of the ideas put forwards by members of investigation groups in these sorts of cases, only add fuel to the fire. For example, news outlet *Bedfordshire Live* quoted a member of the Anglia Paranormal Investigation Society as saying that "there's definitely something strange going on at the church, and my personal view is that it's down to black magic practices held there. I think it's possible for a group of satanists to conjure up something and leave it behind. A sort of guardian or elemental. If this is the case it certainly does its job because it frightens the living daylights out of people."

While there is no evidence that such a thing has been taking place outside of conjecture and this is someone's personal opinion, it is very easy to see how such claims can fan the flames.

As you might expect with all this activity taking place, myths and superstitious beliefs have arisen surrounding Clophill. These include the claim that the church is oriented incorrectly, and so has opened its doors to Hell because it faces away from God. Most churches since the eighth century have an east-west orientation. The congregation faces the rising sun, symbolising Christ as the light of the world.

Whilst it is the case that the orientation at Clophill was the other way around, this is in fact not unusual, and many other churches are laid out in this way. The reasoning is usually a combination of factors which can include landscape topography, building structure needs, and others. In more recent years, many churches have elected to have the priest celebrate at the altar facing west rather than east, and none of them seem to have been overtaken by demonic forces just yet.

It has also been claimed that the church was built on the remains of a leper hospital which used to be presided over by monks in the area. There has never been any evidence found for this, and it is possible that this has come about from a misunderstanding that the land on which the church has been built is called Deadman's Hill. In fact, this is a different piece of ground adjacent to the A6 road, where two years before the first Clophill desecration, in 1961, a man named Michael Gregsten was killed. Another man, James Hanratty, was charged with the murder, found guilty, and was hanged for the crime, but many believe that he was innocent. There is no connection with the site of St Mary's Church.

However, notable stories can easily become conflated in this way, elements become combined and, much like the results of ostension, new narratives are formed which then become taken as accurate. This is how folklore works, and why it is such a fascinating subject which is ingrained in so much of our everyday lives, as hopefully this exploration of the church from a folkloric perspective has demonstrated.

Afterword and Acknowledgements

As the last paragraph of the closing chapter says, I hope that you've found this exploration into some of the folklore connected with the hallowed ground of our churches and churchyards interesting.

"Some" is an important word here. Folklore is a subject that is stuffed full of rabbit holes, and the more you dig, the more you find that the rabbits have dug more and more warrens that you can disappear down. A broad overview volume such as this one can only ever give a flavour. I hope mine has done that, and I hope that maybe you will go down a few rabbit holes of your own, looking into some of the subjects in more detail. If you do, I will always be delighted to hear about what you've found, and I'm very easy to contact online through *The Folklore Podcast* website and social media.

I have so much material on my own research spreadsheets that I have not used, but I couldn't bring you everything. Sometimes, this was just to limit the number of examples of a particular thing. Sometimes, I didn't use a story purely because I couldn't fit it easily into the flow of the narrative and the subjects that the book addressed. That's why I started this afterword...just so I could slip a couple more in!

For example, I regret not being able to include the fact that in 2003, whilst construction workers were building the Eurostar rail link to Kings Cross St Pancras station in London, they came across the remains of a walrus that had been buried in a nineteenth-century churchyard belonging to St Pancras Church. The walrus wasn't just put into the ground…it was in a coffin, along with more human remains.

It is impossible to say for certain how the walrus came to be in the coffin. It seems unlikely that it was the coffin occupant's favourite pet and they couldn't let it go. More probably, it was used for some sort of medical reason and was then buried along with human cadavers that had been used for the same purpose.

I was equally sorry not to be able to discuss All Saint's Church at Haggerston, in the London Borough of Hackney. Here, on the first Sunday in February, professional clowns attend to honour Joseph Grimaldi. Those in the congregation wear their full clown attire and are fully made-up, and they put on a public performance at the end of the service.

Grimaldi's grave is located in a park in Islington which is named after the famous clown. Close by are two more "graves" dedicated to Grimaldi and the man who first employed him, Charles Dibdin. These are actually artworks on which people are invited to dance.

There are many other graves and headstones with curious symbols, messages, and other oddities waiting to be discovered. Seek them out and see what you can find.

I am indebted to a number of people who have made this book what it is. First and foremost, the biggest thank you has to go to Tracy Nicholas, host of the *Folkloring* podcast, who has also been a correspondent on my own podcast for some time. Tracy works closely with the publisher Crossed Crow Books and was particularly interested in the subject matter when this book was commissioned. She asked me if I would like help in researching some of the folklore, primarily from the US angle originally, as she is based in the States.

From this, the giant spreadsheets were born! Tracy fell down all of those rabbit holes which I referred to at the start of this section and, before she knew it, and to my great surprise, there was suddenly a mass of material to draw on. As time passed, she asked if she could look up more. I would have been stupid to say no. To me, the ethos of folklore as a subject is in the sharing of material.

Tracy's research helped to flesh out many portions of this book and sent me onto other research paths that I probably would not have gone down otherwise. I could not be more grateful. She is writing a book for Crossed Crow herself as I write this, and I hope I can help out in some way to repay the debt.

Thanks also to all the many other people who have, either knowingly or unknowingly, contributed to this text. I've drawn on sources, ancient and modern, printed and online. Sometimes even a random Tweet has added a new piece of research. That's how the pudding bell came to be included. Other people have answered my direct questions to clarify points. I thank all of them for enriching the work.

Finally, I thank Blake Malliway and all the staff at Crossed Crow for bringing this book to the world. They are a pleasure to work with in every way, and I hope that I shall have the opportunity to continue to do so. Especially as I keep pestering them to add more folklore to their excellent occult catalogue!

It was in a Devon coffee shop on one of his trips to the UK that I first had the pleasure of sitting down to chat to Blake, and it was then that I discovered that he wanted a tame folklorist to write him a book on church folklore. I thought this was a great idea, and I'd wanted for some time to have the opportunity to work with a decent publisher in the US. The rest is history.

Finally, thanks to you, the reader, for choosing this book. Maybe you have read some of my other books or listened to my podcast. If not, maybe now you will consider it. Maybe you wanted to learn more about the intersection between churches and folklore. Or maybe you just loved the wonderful cover. Whatever your reason for choosing this book, I thank you for doing so.

SELECT BIBLIOGRAPHY

The following selected bibliography comprises the main books and websites used in the compilation of the research for this title.

BOOKS

Andrews, William. *Old Church Lore*. The Hull Press, 1891.

Briggs, Katharine. *British Folk Tales*. Pantheon Books (Random House), 1977.

Burton, Alfred. *Rush-Bearing*. Legare Street Press, 2023.

Cabell Djabri, S. *The Story of the Sepulchre*. Shamrock Press, 1989.

Castleton, David. *Church Curiosities: Strange objects and bizarre legends*. Shire Publications, 2021.

Charubel. *Psychology of Botany: A Treatise on Trees, Shrubs and Plants*. R. Welch, 1906.

Culpeper, Nicholas. *Culpeper's English Physician*. London, 1789.

Dart, John. *Westmonasterium Or the History and Antiquities of the Abbey Church of St. Peters Westminster*. James Cole, 1723.

Folkard, Richard. *Plant Lore, Legends and Lyrics*. R. Folkard and Son, 1884.

Frost, Arnold. *The Ballad of the Wind, the Devil and Lincoln Minster.* J.W. Ruddock, 1906.

Greenoak, Francesca. *God's Acre. The Flowers and Animals of the Parish Church.* Orbis Publishing Ltd., 1985.

Hageneder, Fred. *Yew.* Reaktion Books, 2023.

Harte, Jeremy. *Cloven Country: The Devil and the English Landscape.* Reaktion Books, 2022.

Henderson, William. *Notes on the folk-lore of the northern counties of England and the borders.* Folk-lore Society, 1879.

King, Graham. *The British Book of Spells and Charms.* Troy Books, 2016.

Kruse, John T. *A Guide to Lore, Magic and World of the Good Folk.* Llewellyn Publications, 2020.

Kvideland, Reimund and Henning K. Sehmsdorf. *Scandinavian Folk Belief and Legend.* University of Minnesota Press, 1988.

Lanctot, Barbara. *A Walk Through Graceland Cemetery. A Chicago Architecture Foundation Walking Tour.* Chicago Architecture Foundation, 1992.

Maxwell Wood, J. *Witchcraft and Superstitious Record in the South-Western District of Scotland.* J. Maxwell & Son, 1911.

Maynard, Christopher. *The World of the Unknown: Ghosts.* Usborne, 1977.

Noble, Thomas, editor. *The History of the County of Derby.* Henry Mozley and Son, 1829.

Norman, Mark. *Black Dog Folklore.* Troy Books, 2015.

—. *The Folklore of Devon.* Exeter Press, 2023.

—. *Zoinks! The Spooky Folklore Behind Scooby Doo.* Oak Tree Books, 2024.

Norman, Mark & Tracey Norman. *Dark Folklore.* The History Press, 2021.

Ochota, Mary-Ann. *Secret Britain: Unearthing our Mysterious Past.* Frances Lincoln, 2020.

Richardson, Moses A. *The Local Historian's Table Book.* J.R. Smith, 1846.

Sayer, Sylvia. *The Outline of Dartmoor's Story.* S.T. Elson, 1951.

Snider, Tui. *Understanding Cemetery Symbols.* Castle Azle Press, 2017.

Simpson, Jacqueline & Steve Roud. *A Dictionary of English Folklore*. Oxford, 2003.

Thorpe, Benjamin. *Northern Mythology*. E. Lumley, 1851–1852.

Tibbits, Charles John. *Folk-lore and Legends: Scotland*. W.W. Gibbings, 1889.

Vaux, Rev. J Edward. *Church Folklore*. Griffith Farran & Co, 1894.

Westwood, Jennifer & Jacqueline Simpson. *The Lore of the Land: A Guide to England's Legends*. Penguin, 2005.

Wright, James. *Historic Building Mythbusting*. The History Press, 2024.

Zappaterra, Yolanda. *Cities of the Dead – The World's Most Beautiful Cemeteries*. Frances Lincoln, 2022.

WEBSITES

"A Guide to Meadows and Wildflowers in Burial Grounds." Pamphlet. *Caring for God's Acre, The Prince of Wales's Charitable Fund*, www.caringforgodsacre.org.uk/wp-content/uploads/2022/06/A-Guide-to-Meadows-and-Wildflowers-in-Burial-Grounds.pdf

"Alice Flagg's Grave." *Atlas Obscura*, www.atlasobscura.com/places/alice-flagg-s-grave

"Anchoring their Communities: How Church Buildings are Bringing People Together." *University of Birmingham*, www.birmingham.ac.uk/news/2023/anchoring-their-communities-how-church-buildings-are-bringing-people-together

Barkan, Jonathan. "10 Terrifying Folklore Creatures From Around the World." *Bloody-Disgusting*, bloody-disgusting.com/the-further/3415486/10-terrifying-folklore-creatures-around-world/

"The Bogie and Stowe Church." *Fairyist, The Fairy Investigation Society*, www.fairyist.com/fairy-tales/the-bogie-and-stowe-church/

Bolton, Josh. "The abandoned Bedfordshire church that's 'one of the county's most haunted building' after use of black magic." *Bedfordshire Live*, www.bedfordshirelive.co.uk/news/history/abandoned-bedfordshire-church-thats-one-5771331

Burne, Charlotte S. "The 'Devil's Door' in Wroxhall Abbey Church." *Folklore*, vol. 19, no. 4, 1908, pp. 458–59. *JSTOR*, www.jstor.org/stable/1254239.

Bryant, James. "Campanology." James Bryant, Pd.D., *University of Texas at Austin*, www.bio.utexas.edu/faculty/bryant/personal/campanology.html

Carpenter, Nicola. "Clophill Church: A Guide to Hauntings and Myths." *Spooky Isles*, www.spookyisles.com/haunted-clophill-church/

Carter, Jake. "Church Grim: Guardian Dog Spirit Who Protects the Churchyard From Evil." *Anomalien*, anomalien.com/church-grim-guardian-dog-spirit-who-protects-the-churchyard-from-evil/

Castleton, David. "7 Really Weird Objects in British Churchyards." *The Serpent's Pen*, www.davidcastleton.net/british-churchyards-weird-objects-standing-stones/

—. "The Strange Cauldron of Frensham Church, a White Witch & the Devil." *The Serpent's Pen*, www.davidcastleton.net/cauldron-frensham-church-mother-ludlams-cave/

"Catholic Funeral Traditions." *Everplans*, ewww.everplans.com/articles/catholic-funeral-traditions

"Cemetery and Graveyard Trees: Folklore, Superstition and History." *TalkDeath*, www.talkdeath.com/cemetery-graveyard-trees-folklore-supersitition-history/

"Chesterfield's Crooked Spine." *Atlas Obscura*, www.atlasobscura.com/places/chesterfields-crooked-spire

"Church Grims." *Astonishing Legends*, astonishinglegends.com/astonishing-legends/2018/10/17/church-grims

Connolly, Lawrence C. "Mystery Theatre Supplement: The Strange History of Devil's Doors." *The 21st-Century Scoop*, lawrencecconnolly.com/2021/10/11/dd/

"Corpse Roads." *Engole*, engole.info/corpse-roads/

"Devil's Door." *Engole*, engole.info/devils-door/

"Devil's Knell." *Engole*, engole.info/devils-knell/

"The Devil Head of Raus Church." *Atlas Obscura,* www.atlasobscura.com/places/devil-head-of-raus-church

"The Devil's Fingerprints." *Atlas Obscura,* www.atlasobscura.com/places/the-devils-fingerprints

"The Devil's Stone." *Atlas Obscura,* www.atlasobscura.com/places/the-devils-stone-lubeck-germany

"Edinburgh Honours Greyfriars Bobby at Commemorative Ceremony." *History Scotland,* www.historyscotland.com/history/edinburgh-honours-greyfriars-bobby-at-commemorative-ceremony/

Esparza, Daniel. *"The Day the Architect of a Church Tricked the Devil." Aleteia,* aleteia.org/2017/02/15/the-day-the-architect-of-a-church-tricked-the-devil

Farber, Jessie Lie. "Symbolism on Gravestones." *The Association for Gravestone Studies,* gravestonestudies.org/knowledge-center/symbolism#faqnoanchor

"Flaying to the Mainland from Rathlin (Co. Antrim)." *Fairyist, The Fairy Investigation Society,* www.fairyist.com/fairy-tales/flying-to-the-mainland-from-rathlin-co-antrim/

Flight, Tim. "10 of the Creepiest Stories from English Folklore." *History Collection,* historycollection.com/10-of-the-creepiest-stories-from-english-folklore/

—. "The Devil's in the Detail: 16 Stories of Satan Sprinkled Throughout the Pages of World History." *History Collection,* historycollection.com/the-devils-in-the-detail-16-stories-of-satan-sprinkled-throughout-the-pages-of-world-history/

Fowler, Julian. "Ancient Fermanagh Cure Gets Modern Makeover." *BBC News,* www.bbc.com/news/uk-northern-ireland-46651702

Gates, Henry Louis Jr. "How the Black Church Saved Black America." *The Harvard Gazette,* news.harvard.edu/gazette/story/2021/03/the-history-and-importance-of-the-black-church/. Excerpt from *The Black Church: This is Our Story, This is Our Song* (Penguin, 2021).

Gazur, Ben. "10 Medieval Tales of the Devil." *Listverse,* listverse.com/2017/10/23/10-medieval-tales-of-the-devil/

Graveyardbridge (administrator). "Watching for the Nearly Departed on St. Mark's Eve." *What Lies Beyond* message boards, April 24 2020, whatliesbeyond.boards.net/thread/10973/watching-nearly-departed-marks-eve

Gray, Thomas. "Elegy Written in a Country Churchyard." *Poetry Foundation,* www.poetryfoundation.org/poems/44299/elegy-written-in-a-country-churchyard

"Grimaldi's Grave." *London Remembers,* www.londonremembers.com/memorials/grimaldi-s-grave

"The Hadstock 'Daneskin'– new research on an old mystery." *Saffron Walden Museum,* www.saffronwaldenmuseum.org/2022/04/27/the-hadstock-daneskin-new-research-on-an-old-mystery/

Harper, Audrey. "Creepin' It Real: The Church Grim." *The Sandy River Review,* sandyriverreview.com/2019/02/20/creepin-it-real-the-church-grim/

"Hand of St. Etheldreda." *Atlas Obscura,* www.atlasobscura.com/places/relic-of-st-etheldreda

"The Haunted St. Michael's Church." *Ghost City Tours,* ghostcitytours.com/chicago/haunted-chicago/st-michaels-church/

Heatherson, Liam. "Canewdon Church & Superstition." *Beyond the Point,* beyondthepoint.co.uk/canewdon-gaols-ghosts-ghouls/

"He Loves Me, He Loves Me Not: 10 Valentine's Day Superstitions You Never Knew." *Appleyard Flowers,* www.appleyardflowers.com/flowerdiaries/valentines-day-superstitions/

"Holy Lance." *Encyclopedia Britannica,* www.britannica.com/topic/Holy-Lance

Ian. "St Mark's Eve." *Mysterious Britain & Ireland: Mysteries, Legends & the Paranormal,* www.mysteriousbritain.co.uk/festivals/st-marks-eve/

Johnson, Steve and Rose Nightingale, guests. "Superstition." *Fun With Bells,* Association of Ringing Teachers, funwithbells.com/transcript-for-superstition/

Laity, Kathy. "Celtic saints with names beginning L-N." *Celtic Glory,* www.celticglory.com/history/celtic-saints-names-beginning-l-n

Leah, Heather. "Old Burying Ground: 300-year-old cemetery is one of the oldest in NC." *WRAL News,* www.wral.com/story/old-burying-ground-300-year-old-cemetery-is-one-of-the-oldest-in-nc/19793516/

"The Legend of the Evil Rider." *Dartmoor National Park,* www.dartmoor.gov.uk/learning/dartmoor-legends/the-legend-of-the-evil-rider

Lennox, Suzie. "Why Are There Cages Over Graves? It's Not For Vampires!" *My Macabre Road Trip,* mymacabreroadtrip.com/cages-over-graves/

Lennox, Suzie. "The Cursed Grave of Seath Mor Sgorfhiaclach." *My Macabre Road Trip,* mymacabreroadtrip.com/the-cursed-grave-of-seath-mor/

Lidz, Franz. "Soil From a Northern Ireland Graveyard May Lead Scienstists to a Powerful New Antibiotic." *Smithsonian Magazine,* www.smithsonianmag.com/science-nature/astonishing-medical-potential-soil-northern-ireland-graveyard-180973741/

Luksic, Nicola. "How Jesus' foreskin became one of Christianity's most-coveted relics — and then disappeared." *CBC/Radio-Canada,* www.cbc.ca/radio/ideas/how-jesus-foreskin-became-one-of-christianity-s-most-coveted-relics-and-then-disappeared-1.6002421

Mander, Joe. "St. Clement's Church & The Cutlass Stone." *Beyond the Point,* beyondthepoint.co.uk/st-celements-church-the-cutlass-stone/

"Mermaid Chair." *Atlas Obscura,* www.atlasobscura.com/places/mermaid-of-zennor-chair

Minster, Christopher. "Ecuadorian Legend: The Story of Cantuña and the Devil." *ThoughtCo.,* www.thoughtco.com/ecuadorian-legend-the-story-of-cantuna-2136635

"Misericord." *Engole,* engole.info/misericord/
"Mistletoe – 1." *Plant-Lore,* www.plant-lore.com/plantofthemonth/mistletoe-1/
"Mountain Churches." *National Churches Trust,* www.nationalchurchestrust.org/explore/story/mountains
Nicholas, Dean. "Walrus Found in London Grave." The Londonist, londonist.com/2013/07/walrus-found-in-london-grave
Nuwer, Rachel. "Meet the Fantastically Bejeweled Skeletons of Catholicism's Forgotten Martyrs." *Smithsonian Magazine,* www.smithsonianmag.com/history/meet-the-fantastically-bejeweled-skeletons-of-catholicisms-forgotten-martyrs-284882/
"Outgoing Outsides." *National Churches Trust,* www.nationalchurchestrust.org/explore/why/outgoing-outsides
"Palm." *Plant-Lore,* www.plant-lore.com/plantofthemonth/palm-sunday/
Perkins, Wayne. "Up On the Roof: Shoe Outline Graffiti." *Ritual Protection Marks & Ritual Practices,* ritualprotectionmarks.com/2023/12/02/up-on-the-roof-shoe-outline-graffiti/
—. "A Discovery of Angels: How an Anglo-Saxon Chapel Gave up Its Secrets." *Ritual Protection Marks & Ritual Practices,* ritualprotectionmarks.com/2022/12/23/a-discovery-of-angels-how-an-anglo-saxon-chapel-gave-up-its-secrets/
Postrado, Alex. "Kyrkogrim (Church Grim): Canine Protectors of the Dead." *Lorethrill: Fables and Legends,* lorethrill.com/kyrkogrim-church-grim-sacrificial-dogs/
"Relic." *Encyclopedia Britannica,* www.britannica.com/topic/relic
"The Relic Chapel at the Church of the Most Holy Redeemer." *Atlas Obscura,* www.atlasobscura.com/places/the-relic-chapel-at-the-church-of-the-most-holy-redeemer-new-york-new-york
Rhys, Dani. "18 Powerful Pagan Symbols & Their Meanings." *SymbolSage,* symbolsage.com/pagan-symbols-list/
—. "Ichthys Symbolism: From Pagan Origins to Christianity." *SymbolSage,* symbolsage.com/ichthys-symbol/

—. "The Triskelion: From Celtic Roots to Modern Interpretations." *SymbolSage,* symbolsage.com/triskelion-symbol-meaning/

Royvickery (user). "Church decorations at Advent." *Plant-Lore,* www.plant-lore.com/news/church-decorations-at-advent/

—. "Red & white flowers on New Church Day." *Plant-Lore,* www.plant-lore.com/news/red-and-white-flowers-on-new-church-day/

Roldan, Karen. "What Is a Death Knell? How to Toll the Funeral Bells." *USurns Online,* www.usurnsonline.com/funerals/death-knell/

"Scottish Traditions: Lammas Day." *History Scotland,* www.historyscotland.com/history/scottish-traditions-lammas-day/

Sedgwick, Icy. "The Folklore of Time: Clocks, Calendars, and Church Bells." *Folklore Blog,* www.icysedgwick.com/folklore-of-time/

—. "The Not So Holy Ghost: England's Haunted Churches." *Folklore Blog,* www.icysedgwick.com/haunted-churches/

—. "For Whom the Bell Tolls: Folklore of Churches and Churchyards." *Folklore Blog,* www.icysedgwick.com/folklore-of-churches/

Sheppard-Reynolds, Jessica. "The Corpse-Devouring Hyena of the Medieval Bestiary." *Getty Research Foundation Museum,* blogs.getty.edu/iris/the-corpse-devouring-hyena-of-the-medieval-bestiary/

SMacB (user). "A Witch story—St Michael and All Angels—Edmondthorpe, Leicestershire." *Waymarking,* www.waymarking.com/waymarks/WMYXQ1_A_Witch_story_St_Michael_and_All_Angels_Edmondthorpe_Leicestershire

"Spring Flowers." *National Churches Trust,* www.nationalchurchestrust.org/explore/story/spring-flowers

Stolze, Dolly. "The Skeletal Remains of a Hellhound in the Folklore of Devil Dogs." *Atlas Obscura,* www.atlasobscura.com/articles/archaeology-folklore-and-the-skeletal-remains-of-a-hellhound

"Stained-Glass Demons." *Atlas Obscura*, www.atlasobscura.com/places/stained-glass-demons-strasbourg-cathedral

"St. John's Church." *Atlas Obscura*, www.atlasobscura.com/places/st-johns-church-glynn

"St Catherine." *National Churches Trust*, www.nationalchurchestrust.org/church/st-catherine-ludham

"St Govan Chapel." *National Churches Trust*, www.nationalchurchestrust.org/church/st-govan-chapel-bosherston

"St Issui." *National Churches Trust*, www.nationalchurchestrust.org/church/st-issui-patricio

"St Peris." *National Churches Trust*, www.nationalchurchestrust.org/church/st-peris-nant-peris

"St Newlina's fig tree." *Plant-Lore*, www.plant-lore.com/plantofthemonth/st-newlinas-fig-tree/

Swansea University. "Bacteria found in ancient Irish soil halts growth of superbugs: New hope for tackling antibiotic resistance." *ScienceDaily*, www.scotlands-yew-trees.org/history-culture-myth/the-churchyard-yew-a-poem

Tetrault, Sam. "10 Cemetery Superstitions from Around the World." *Cake*, www.joincake.com/blog/cemetery-superstitions/

Quinn, Gerry and Paul Dyson. "Bacteria Discovered in Ancient Irish 'Healing' Soil Halts Growth of Antibiotic-Resistant Superbugs." *Newsweek*, www.newsweek.com/antibiotic-resistance-superbug-ancient-soil-bacteria-ireland-streptomyces-1283324

Wallace, P.J. "The Origins of the Lychgate." *Somerset and Bath Paranormal*, www.somersetandbathparanormal.co.uk/the-origins-of-the-lychgate

"The Wax-Encased Remains of Blessed Anna Maria Taigi." *Atlas Obscura*, www.atlasobscura.com/places/the-waxencased-remains-of-blessed-anna-maria-taigi-rome-italy

Wells, Michael. "Does a 19th Century Priest Haunt St. Mary's Episcopal Church? KCQ Goes Ghost Hunting." *Kansas City Public Library*, kchistory.org/blog/

does-19th-century-priest-haunt-st-mary%E2%80%99s-episcopal-church-kcq-goes-ghost-hunting

"'The Wisdom of Solomon' Stone Pyramid." *Atlas Obscura,* www.atlasobscura.com/places/wisdom-of-solomon-stone-pyramid-annes-limehouse-church

Wright, William J. "Creepy Tales of Haunted Churches." *Grunge,* www.grunge.com/232327/creepy-tales-of-haunted-churches/

Zhelyazkov, Yordan. "Celtic Dragon—Mythology, Meaning and Symbolism." *SymbolSage,* symbolsage.com/celtic-dragon-mythology-meaning/

—. "The Green Man: Symbolism, Origins, and Cultural Significance." *SymbolSage,* symbolsage.com/history-of-the-green-man/